THE LITERACY COACH'S GAME PLAN

Making Teacher Collabora...
and School Improv...

aya Sadder and Gabrielle Nidus

INTERNATIONAL Reading Association

800 Barksdale Road, PO Box 8139
Newark, DE 19714-8139, USA
www.reading.org

The International Reading Association attempts, through its publications, to provide a forum for a wide spectrum of opinions on reading. This policy permits divergent viewpoints without implying the endorsement of the Association.

Executive Editor, Books   Corinne M. Mooney
Developmental Editor   Charlene M. Nichols
Developmental Editor   Tori Mello Bachman
Developmental Editor   Stacey L. Reid
Editorial Production Manager   Shannon T. Fortner
Design and Composition Manager   Anette Schuetz

Project Editors   Stacey L. Reid and Rebecca A. Fetterolf

Art   Cover design: Brad Tillinghast; Cover photography: (large background image) ©iStockphoto.com/Helder Almeida, (boxed images from top left) ©iStockphoto.com/Catherine Yeulet, ©iStockphoto.com/Catherine Yeulet, Gabrielle Nidus and Maya Sadder, ©iStockphoto.com/ Catherine Yeulet, Gabrielle Nidus and Maya Sadder, ©iStockphoto.com/Chris Schmidt, Gabrielle Nidus and Maya Sadder; Interior photography: (pp. 33, 36, 45, 77, 115) Gabrielle Nidus and Maya Sadder

Copyright 2009 by the International Reading Association, Inc.
All rights reserved. No part of this publication may be reproduced or transmitted in any form or by any means, electronic or mechanical, including photocopy, or any information storage and retrieval system, without permission from the publisher.

The publisher would appreciate notification where errors occur so that they may be corrected in subsequent printings and/or editions.

Library of Congress Cataloging-in-Publication Data
Sadder, Maya.
  The literacy coach's game plan : making teacher collaboration, student learning, and school improvement a reality / Maya Sadder and Gabrielle Nidus.
    p. cm.
  Includes bibliographical references and index.
  ISBN 978-0-87207-697-6
  1. Language arts teachers--In-service training--United States. 2. Language arts--United States. 3. Reading--United States. I. Nidus, Gabrielle. II. Title.
  LB1576.S223 2009
  372.6'044--dc22
                                                                        2009028278

SUSTAINABLE
FORESTRY
INITIATIVE

Certified Fiber Sourcing
www.sfiprogram.org

The emancipator unbinds our fetters
And brings hope to conquer fear.
The educator frees minds with letters
And expands life's scope beyond our sphere.
                                        —Dr. Bernard Nidus

To Lucy "Bahoo" Elliott, for infinity and beyond

And to Isaac Geoffrey Shor for teaching me to see the joy
in a world I thought I already knew

CONTENTS

Maya Sadder brings years of experience from Chicago Public Schools in Chicago, Illinois, USA, working primarily with intermediate and upper-grade students. As a classroom teacher, she has inspired her students to reach their greatest potential and consistently helped them achieve high levels of academic performance. She has written and received numerous grants to support the learning environment while a classroom teacher and has been the recipient of several awards including the Outstanding Teaching Achievement Award, North Lawndale Community Teaching Award, and the award for teaching excellence in her district area. She was also selected to represent her school at Yale University through the Youth Guidance Comer School Network.

As a literacy coach, she has helped lead a schoolwide literacy reform effort based on an organic balanced literacy framework at National Teachers Academy in Chicago. She has organized, created, and delivered hundreds of hours of high-quality professional development and engaging workshops for teachers. Her literacy expertise and practice has enabled her to conduct professional development through the International Reading Association and other respected professional organizations across the United States and abroad. Maya holds a bachelor's degree in elementary education and master's degrees in curriculum and instruction as well as educational leadership and supervision. She is currently enrolled in a doctoral program at Loyola University in Chicago.

Gabrielle Nidus has been motivating students to excel as readers and writers and inspiring teachers to flourish as literacy leaders for over a decade in New York City and Chicago Public Schools. Her experience as a classroom teacher runs the gamut from early childhood education to high school. Gabrielle's innovative lesson plans have been published by Scholastic and the Do Something Social Action Network. She has conducted numerous professional development workshops for educators across the country on improving student literacy at multiple levels. In her work as a computer integration consultant, she has enhanced classroom experiences with new technologies. As a literacy coach at the National Teachers Academy, a Chicago Public Schools professional development academy, she continues to support teachers, using student work as the foundation of her coaching.

Gabrielle holds a bachelor's degree from Brown University. In addition, she has a master's degree in English education from Teachers College, Columbia University, and a master's degree in education, communication, and technology from New York University.

Author Information for Correspondence and Workshops

If you have coaching ideas you'd like to share with us or questions you'd like to ask about coaching, please contact Maya and Gabrielle through our website at www.formativecoaching.com or by e-mail at lc@formativecoaching.com. As you use the ideas in the book, we hope you'll also let us know how they work in your schools.

PREFACE

As literacy coaches at National Teachers Academy (NTA), a large urban neighborhood school on Chicago's South Side, we decided to write this book to share some of the strategies we have used in our work with teachers to build a professional learning community focused on student achievement. Too often in our careers, we had felt that our coaching of teachers had been fully dictated by the swing of the educational pendulum. As a result, the process of adult learning frequently felt as random as a game of bingo. Our districts or schools chose an instructional method to promote, we provided professional development on the topic, and, if the instructional method matched with their repertoires, teachers might insert it into their teaching with a mild hint of enthusiasm. Meaningful discourse. Think, pair, share. Bingo! If the advice or teaching method did not seemingly fit, it was quickly discarded and the game continued. However, we knew, like many schools, that we did not have time for meaningless games.

We dutifully met with teachers, but our coaching conversations often felt awkward. Having received no instruction on how to work with adult learners, we were unsure of how to proceed. What should we talk about during our meetings? Was it our role to tell teachers if we thought a particular strategy was effective, or should we keep our conversations solely focused on suggestions? We wondered how we could develop workshops that would translate into higher student achievement. And what was our responsibility in providing leadership for literacy instruction in our school?

Searching for "The Way In"

In our first years at NTA, we proceeded cautiously. We met with teachers and modeled our professional development sessions after the ones we had seen before. We chose topics that we thought were important, created workshops that we felt were engaging and research-based, and then held our breath, hoping teachers would incorporate our suggestions. We knew there was something valuable about meeting as a whole school to discuss literacy; however, the feedback teachers gave us was that they wanted more time to plan as a grade level. And yet, each year, no matter how much preparation the teacher did the year before, students continued to struggle with the same problems. Why was it that fourth graders did not understand how to use paragraphs when they had learned about them since first grade? Why were sixth graders still unclear about what an inference was when we had seen lessons on the topic throughout the intermediate cycle?

We knew we had to have these difficult conversations as a staff, and yet, when we tried, we often became mired down in discussing problems that we, as teachers, could not solve. It was the parents' fault, society's injustices, too much television or time spent playing video games, or the fact that we did not have an after-school program to help struggling students. We were concerned that these conversations would lead to teachers placing blame on those that came before them. We were concerned that we might hear that it was sixth-grade teachers' fault because they did not require students to reread their writing or that we might hear that it was third-grade teachers' fault for not teaching them how to write essays, or maybe the fault would fall squarely on pre-K teachers.

One thing was clear: Our community was struggling. Teachers felt overwhelmed by the demands of teaching in a high-needs, high-poverty school. They were stressed. Some were willing to try new instructional techniques if they felt like they could help students, while others remained steadfast in their approach—whether it worked or not. The assessments all showed the same thing: Students were not succeeding in the way we hoped they could. Obviously, our workshops and individual meetings with teachers were not providing them with the support they needed to feel competent as instructors and help our students achieve. That's when we called an emergency meeting in the middle of December to meet with the principal to rework our literacy plan. What emerged was a new definition of our role as literacy coaches and a vision for literacy instruction at our school.

The Door Opens

The analysis of student work became the foundation of our schoolwide professional development time, our coaching sessions, and our grade-level meetings. All along, we had been looking for a way to understand how students were progressing, to make clear and public grade-level goals to differentiate the curriculum, and ultimately to plot the course of effective instruction. We did not want to wait for state tests to tell us how our students were faring. As we sat in professional development meetings and planning sessions, we began to notice how teachers would often bring student work, piles of Venn diagrams, mountains of reading journals, and armies of essays that they hoped to look at during a break. As we watched the teachers strum through the papers, we noticed them pointing out particular parts of an essay to a nearby teacher, smiling, looking quizzically, making notes, and deeply investigating the work before them. Teachers wanted to look at their students' work and gauge student understanding, but knowing how to do this and use the information not solely for a grade but to plan effectively was challenging. The answer to how to engage teachers in professional development, facilitate collaboration, and assist them in and out of the classroom in planning was all around us: in the work of our students. Learning how to understand and use this work to help our students became the focus of our literacy coaching and the foundation of our learning community. When teachers gathered together to talk about instruction, they met with evidence of student learning in hand.

As we started to incorporate the analysis of student work into our coaching and professional development, we noticed profound effects on the way teachers began to talk about curriculum and instruction in addition to their desire to collaborate with one another. Our coaching sessions became focused on student achievement; our talk was concrete, less about blame and more about joint investigation. Sitting with teachers, looking at a running record, we were a team of researchers, developing techniques for analyzing what we saw, coming up with hypotheses about how to help students, and reflecting on the efficacy of our instruction (see Figure 1, which illustrates how student work, combined with aspects of collaborative analysis of that work, provides the way in for both coach and teacher).

We wrote this book to help coaches find "the way in" to building a school culture where meaningful discussions about effective instruction are based on data and, most of all, are a part of day-to-day practice. Above all, we wanted it to be real—to talk about the challenges coaches face as

Figure 1. Student Work as the Way In

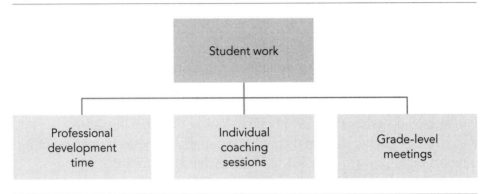

they negotiate the rocky terrain of adult learning and provide systems and structures coaches can use to build and maintain a school culture focused on student results.

How to Use This Book

We know that literacy coaches are busy people, occupying a variety of roles: from reading teacher, to resource room, to librarian, to grant writer, and even to lunchroom monitor. Some coaches work in one school, while others are in charge of professional development across many different buildings and content areas. And, all along, the coach must find a balance between the activities that populate their everyday schedule and the ones they know are truly a part of affecting school change. We wrote this book so that you can either read it chapter by chapter or choose the parts that pertain to where you are in your coaching.

Chapter 1, "Preseason," provides a rationale for developing a school culture around the analysis of student work and how this data can help tie together the many different responsibilities of the literacy coach. In this chapter, you will learn about what a literacy coach does and explore your enthusiasm and fears about coaching.

Chapter 2, "Stepping Onto the Playing Field," illustrates steps and techniques for effective coaching and supports the coach in creating a game plan for working with individual teachers. Through this chapter, you can find ways to begin to form relationships with teachers and learn more about how to go about taking a survey of the type of data your school has available.

Chapter 3, "The Game Plan," delves deeper by providing specific strategies for looking and making sense of student work. You will learn how to find trends in a class's work and discover a method to help set goals based on the work of individual students.

Chapter 4, "Batter Up!" examines techniques for coaches to make their time with teachers meaningful, differentiated, and focused on student achievement. In this chapter, you will learn how to investigate techniques to collect data on your classroom visits and collaborate with a teacher to instruct a class.

Chapter 5, "The Huddle: Developing the Professional Learning Community," demonstrates techniques and strategies to strengthen your professional learning community to support student achievement and professional development at your school.

Chapter 6, "Establishing a Winning Record: Coaching for School Change," extends this exploration by discussing how coaches can help develop an action plan as a school focused on student achievement through formative data. Specifically, you will learn how to delve deeper and learn about ways to support groups of teachers as they look at student work to influence learning schoolwide.

Finally, in Chapter 7, "The Legacy of Your Coaching," you will learn how to reflect on your success as a literacy coach and make plans for the future by preparing for changes in the role of literacy coaching and considering your legacy as a literacy coach. In addition, in Appendix A, we have included many handouts that you can use to facilitate professional development with the teachers at your school, and in Appendix B, we have included detailed protocols to help navigate your use of the coaching strategies outlined in Chapter 3.

We have used the real names of all coaches who are mentioned and quoted in this book, but all teacher and student names used in this book are pseudonyms and are composite sketches that represent the real teachers, students, and classroom experiences that we have encountered in our work as coaches.

Acknowledgments

Our ideas about coaching are born from our everyday work with our wonderful colleagues at NTA and our principal and friend, Amy Rome. We have learned so much from the tireless dedication of our staff, the innovative lessons they have developed, and their constant drive to become better teachers, learners, and leaders for our students. Each chapter of this book is filled with the energy and spirit of the teachers and students at NTA. We also would like to thank Taffy Raphael for encouraging us to publish our work and the college of education at University of Illinois at Chicago for imparting a wealth of knowledge about effective literacy teaching and learning.

Finally, we acknowledge our loving families, who have helped us through the creation of the book. They have provided us with enthusiasm, support, optimism, and laughter. Many thanks and hugs from Gabrielle to Boris, Isaac, Mom, Dad, and David for their love, support, and silliness. And love from Maya to Santino, Justin, Suga, Pappy, E, and K for inspiring the writer in her.

CHAPTER 1

Preseason

Imagine This!

It is the beginning of a new year and, for you, the start of a new position as a literacy coach. You have always loved teaching reading and writing, and you have mentored teachers before, but the thought of working as the literacy coach is daunting. You know that you will have to coach teachers and prepare professional development for the entire staff that will, in turn, help students become more effective readers and writers. You have worked with teams of teachers before and know that they are a demanding audience—their time is precious and they have no extra to waste. Some of the teachers will be more experienced than you, and some will ask you questions about teaching that you might not have an answer for.

Your principal has charged you with the task of supporting curriculum and instruction throughout the school. He wants grade levels to collaborate, teachers to plan more carefully and to differentiate their instruction, and, mostly, student test scores to improve. "You're the right person for the job," he says with a smile. "I know you can do it. Now go for it." That's all the preparation you are going to get for now. You feel a pit in your stomach, despite his confidence. You can't back out now. You look at the list of teachers and read their names out loud. Right now, these are just names; soon these will be people and personalities. You take a deep breath and think to yourself, "How can I show teachers that I am there to support them? How can I make a difference? What's the way in?"

Have you ever watched a coach of a sports team prepare for a big game? With a pen in her hand, she studies her game plan and thinks about the individual strengths of her players. In the lockers and on the field, she spends time debriefing with the team and building their confidence through a rousing speech. On the field, you can tell she has spent precious practice time developing a common language among the players. When one teammate calls for a play, the others seamlessly understand. Their strategy is built on their ability to communicate with one another, pass off, block, stand in for, and do whatever else it may call for to win the game. But imagine a softball team where all the players interpreted the catcher's hand signals in their own way. Or how about a football team that didn't quite understand the coach's scribbles in the playbook? How would they communicate the steps necessary to win the game? How would they know when to pass off, to guard, or to rally? Would they ever see victory?

Now imagine a literacy coach preparing for the school year. She may have a game plan also, but as she begins to roll it out, she realizes the goals of individuals on her team are not all aligned. As the year progresses, she begins to see that they are not all striving for the same end. The principal wants to raise test scores. The parents want to see good grades. Ms. A wants to make it through this year. Ms. T wants all her students to be on grade level. Mr. S is focused on teaching public service, and Ms. Z wants just to be left alone. In an effort to understand her team better, the literacy coach makes time to watch the players on the field. She wants to know their strengths and the challenges that they face. With a paper in hand, she watches and jots down pages and pages of notes about teaching and instruction. But what exactly is important information to share with teachers?

In a meeting, the principal asks the teachers how students are doing. Ms. G says her students are reading on grade level, Mr. P says his students read 90 words per minute, Ms. C says the majority have a lexile of 700, and Ms. R is concerned about half her class who read at a level H but lack comprehension. The principal buys a new program, and the coach suggests that the school focus on reading strategies to improve comprehension. So Ms. G interprets this as giving students time to write in their journals. Mr. P focuses on decoding, Ms. C gives them worksheets with multiple-choice questions to practice, and Ms. R focuses on her student conferences. The good-hearted yet unfocused response of the teachers is the result of a team that does not speak a common language of assessment of instruction and therefore cannot collaborate or build on the work done previously.

If we only applied the rule of the playing field to coaching, we could push our schools toward higher achievement. But how do you establish a team that can function together, speaks a common language, and yet holds each other accountable for high standards of teaching? How do you make your time meaningful when you coach teachers either individually or in teams?

When we began our role as coaches at National Teachers Academy (NTA), a large urban school on Chicago's South Side, our only game plan was to improve students' reading and writing. We joined a team that was already in motion, complete with multiple players: students, teachers, administrators, parents, and a literacy program. In the beginning, it seemed all we could do was to hang on as the machine chugged along.

NTA, which had only been open a few years, was experiencing many of the growing pains common to new schools. We jumped into action, meeting with teachers, planning professional development, looking over student scores on standardized tests, and pulling out students to read with or assess. However, even though we were busy throughout the day, there was no focus to connect our various coaching activities. Although we had many polite, informal conversations about literacy instruction where we casually offered suggestions, these ideas were also quickly forgotten. We found ourselves veering away from the uncomfortable conversations of developing a school with a cohesive approach to literacy, and yet, at the same time it was impossible to avoid the fact that our students were not proficient readers and writers.

The smorgasbord of instructional strategies that teachers offered students during their time at NTA was not adding up to them becoming literate. While our days were spent talking with teachers in the classroom, these talks felt disconnected—one session rarely built on the next. We knew we needed a coordinated approach, one that would help us establish a community of teachers who collaborated and reflected on their instruction without assigning blame. We needed a system that would connect the various activities we did throughout the day and build our role as literacy coaches.

We found our game plan—our coordinated approach, our focus— through the collaborative analysis of student work. We used this data as a way to make decisions about teaching and curriculum. This process helped to define our roles, to create a cycle of inquiry and instruction that informed our coaching, and to reify our school community to become one of collaboration and reflection.

As our conversations with teachers became less about blame and more focused on what we could do to help students, we realized we had stumbled upon something unique. We did not need to wait for standardized tests to tell us how we were doing as a school—it was written in the student work. It hung on every bulletin board, filled every journal, and was a part of every literacy program a school might choose. Student work was the way in.

What Do Literacy Coaches Actually Do?

A proliferation in the number of people working as literacy coaches has occurred in response to the daunting task of preparing students for high-stakes tests (Hatch, 2002). Yet, even with an intense interest from the reading community, there has not been much research about coaching (Walpole & Blamey, 2008), and it is hard to distill the effects a literacy coach makes on student achievement because of all the mitigating factors that contribute to student achievement. Yet schools use their hard-earned resources to fund coaching positions because of the belief that professional development is an integral part of a school environment.

Look through books on literacy coaching and you will hear people attempt to describe this varying and confusing role. Coaches must wear many hats. They need to be able to juggle many balls. They are there to put out fires—and sometimes to light them. While on some days coaches need to be teachers, mentors, leaders, and facilitators, on others they function as book buyers, substitute teachers, test coordinators, resource room teachers, disciplinarians, data processors, recess teachers, librarians, curriculum planners, schedulers, and liaisons between schools and districts and universities (Toll, 2005).

Erika Mora, a coach at an elementary school in Chicago, explains that the main task of a literacy coach should be to propel the literacy curriculum forward. Coaches should be prepared to model lessons, meet with grade-level teams, analyze data, ask questions, observe, and support teachers in their classroom instruction. For Erika, this can sometimes mean helping teachers in classroom management by calling parents or talking with students. She explains that sometimes, "You're half coach and half administrator," no matter how hard you try and define yourself as a teacher.

The International Reading Association (IRA) defines literacy coaches in the following way:

> A reading coach or a literacy coach is a reading specialist who focuses on providing professional development for teachers by providing them with the additional support needed to implement various instructional programs and practices. They provide essential leadership for the school's entire literacy program by helping create and supervise a long-term staff development process that supports both the development and implementation of the literacy program over months and years. These individuals need to have experiences that enable them to provide effective professional development for the teachers in their schools. (From www.reading.org/downloads/standards/definitions.pdf)

Although a literacy coach may teach groups of students, the focus of his or her work is on the professional growth of teachers. This type of support might come in the form of workshops, grade-level meetings, individual coaching sessions, or job-embedded learning. Job-embedded learning is professional development that occurs while teachers engage in their daily work of teaching and planning. This type of learning can be done both formally and informally. It is often one of the most meaningful ways to support teachers, since participants learn while engaging in their regular tasks of planning, teaching, and assessing.

As a literacy coach, there are many ways that you can assist a teacher both in and out of the classroom. Joyce and Showers (1995) identify five types of supports for teachers.

1. Theory: Coaches help teachers by bringing in research, articles, notes, and books so that teachers understand the philosophy behind instructional strategies.
2. Demonstration: Coaches provide teachers with the opportunity to see a lesson taught in their classroom.
3. Practice: Coaches can support teachers by working with students in the classroom so that teachers can practice a newly learned skill with their students.
4. Feedback: Coaches can help teachers reflect on their instruction with the focus on what was effective.

5. In-class coaching: Coaches provide teachers with opportunities to work with a coach in their classroom to confront challenges as they might arise and to determine the direction of instruction.

When we examine IRA's standards for middle and high school coaches (they may be found at www.reading.org/downloads/resources/597coaching_standards.pdf), we begin to develop a picture of the challenging and multifaceted role of the coach. While elementary, middle, and high school coaches may strive for the same goal of increasing students' literacy achievement, the middle and high school standards specifically shed light on the flexibility needed by literacy coaches, who must make their knowledge of best literacy practices accessible to teachers from a variety of content areas in order to promote collaboration among staff.

Standard 1: Skillful Collaborators

Today's model of literacy coaching involves leadership and building the teaching capacity of the school as a whole. It involves the coach working with teachers individually and in teams to build the professional learning community and develop an environment of collegiality and collaboration. Coaches are expected to know techniques and work within the time constraints of busy schools to develop systems whereby teachers and coaches can work collaboratively to plan, teach, and reflect on lessons. Coaches also become involved in outreach programs for parents and community. Many coaches run family literacy nights or offer literacy-related trips or contests to broaden students' experiences.

Standard 2: Skillful Job-Embedded Coaches

Much of the job of coaches is done working side by side with a teacher in his or her classroom. Therefore, coaches must be able to coteach, demonstrate lessons, and illustrate how language arts can be integrated into content area instruction. All this assumes that coaches know various techniques and protocols to facilitate their job-embedded work with teachers and have knowledge about how to approach the teaching of literacy through a variety of content areas. Literacy coach Erika Mora explains that she has discovered a number of icebreakers and incentives to help teachers engage with and enjoy professional development. She takes pictures of teachers in action and creates bulletin boards so that people can see what is happening around the building, and she develops author celebration days and literacy nights. Working with adults is like working with any group of learners—it takes time and thoughtfulness to develop ways to engage them and make learning enjoyable.

Standard 3: Skillful Evaluators of Literacy Needs

Literacy coaches must have the specific skills of the reading specialist and be able to support teachers who work with struggling readers. Often coaches are asked to make decisions about literacy materials and other resources based on the needs of teachers and students. That means that coaches must know how to determine what their school needs. This involves a high degree of comfort with data, both descriptive and quantitative, to understand what supports are needed and for whom. Coaches are often asked to chair leadership teams and must know how to facilitate these team meetings so that others become adept at using data to determine the needs of the school.

Standard 4: Skillful Instructional Strategists

Having skills in teaching reading and writing is perhaps one of the most important attributes for literacy coaches to possess. Although coaches do not need to have had experience with each grade level they coach, they must understand the goals of various grades and effective instructional strategies, in addition to being able to provide teachers with developmentally appropriate resources.

The tasks set forth by these standards can be daunting for new and veteran coaches alike. Coaching is more than just mentoring or making suggestions about instruction and more than running workshops for teachers. It is about providing leadership and creating opportunities for teacher professional development and collaboration—all with the intended goal of improving students' reading and writing.

Qualifications: What Do You Need to Be a Successful Coach?

A solid understanding about literacy and literacy learning is one of the most important qualifications of a literacy coach. For example, IRA provides the following guidelines for a course of study to prepare for becoming a literacy coach (although it is clear that not all coaches have this type of training):

- Previous teaching experience
- Master's degree with concentration in reading education
- A minimum of 24 graduate semester hours in reading and language arts and related courses
- An additional six semester hours of supervised practicum experience

So what are the important characteristics that coaches should possess? Based on our research, our experiences as coaches, and our work with teachers and other coaches, we believe literacy coaches need the following in order to be successful:

- Ability to rally people/leadership capacity
- Good communication skills
- Thick skin
- Ability to see the big picture and establish intermediary steps
- Organization skills
- Creative problem-solving skills
- Love of teaching students and working with adult learners
- Patience and reflectiveness
- Multitasking capabilities
- People skills
- Ways to relax and celebrate

While coaches need a firm understanding of literacy, there are many people skills needed as well. Coaching is a social job that involves navigating the tricky landscape of working with adult learners. While it is important to have the academic credentials to be an effective coach, one must also possess effective communication skills. Communicating is more than just simply finding the right words to say but also thinking about how you will convey the knowledge, questions, and feedback that you will share on a daily basis. According to Mehrabian (1972), 7% of a message is communicated through words; 38% through voice, pitch, intonation, and timing; and the remaining 55% through facial expressions and body language. Equally important in the role of the coach is to be an outstanding listener. Often when coaches are engaging in dialogue with teachers, we make sure to keep an open mind and take a second to think before immediately responding to avoid a reactionary response.

Literacy coaches, above all, must enjoy working with others. Very few parts of literacy coaching are done locked away in an office, devoid of teachers and students. Literacy coaches work with individual teachers in their classroom, they interact with students during the day, they collaborate with grade-level teams to analyze student work, and they meet with teachers to develop professional development. Consider the social nature of one literacy coach's day, as explained by an anonymous participant of a survey on coaching we once distributed:

> First, check email to see if something came in that I need to take care of at beginning of day—from the AR Dept of Education. Look at calendar and itinerary to confirm my schedule. Observe or model in classrooms, K–3. Meetings with grade levels K–3 during the week. Follow up in afternoon with planning, scheduling, and meeting with individual teachers. End of day is spent on computer with email, inputting data, and finalizing planning.

In addition, literacy coaches repeatedly articulate the need to develop a thick skin. Very few people are born with a thick skin. More often, it evolves over time, as you begin to understand the importance of not taking everything too personally. Kate Hogan, a curriculum specialist at TEAM (Together Everyone Achieves More) High School, explains the need for coaches to be thick-skinned and persistent: "There may be days that you go home crying," she explains, "but you keep coming back and being persistent." You need to be patient, another coach articulates—you need to recognize that a teacher may have been doing the same thing for 25 years and may need time to change.

Last, coaches need to find ways to decompress. One coach explains,

> The most important emotional habit that I have in my toolkit is celebration. I have learned to celebrate growth in students and take pleasure in watching kids learn and grow (even if the growth is very small). I allow that warm feeling of student success to wash over me and let my students see how overjoyed I am at their success. I also try to keep my sense of humor, and I like to laugh and joke with students and my colleagues. I have learned to take things less personally. Most negative comments made by reluctant

teachers do not bother me. I just redirect them where before I used to take it personally. Also, I have a lot of family support at home and decompress by taking walks with my son and dog or just losing myself in a good book.

As the literacy coach, above all, you are a member of the team. And although at times you may sit on the sidelines, you feel the roller coaster of emotions as vividly as if you were on the field yourself. As you read the next chapters, you will notice the enormity of the role of providing literacy leadership to a school. Finding ways to maintain your sense of equanimity is of utmost importance to your success and to those around you.

Finding Balance in Your Role

A large part of coaching is knowing how best to spend your time. Where is the highest need in your school? Should you work with Mr. P for one week, or should you spend your time focusing on the writing and work with three teachers from the middle school? As you weigh the options, you will realize that coaches are constantly balancing two perspectives: a microscopic view that focuses on an individual classroom or grade and a macroscopic view of the contributions of all the classrooms within the school in making a student literate. This telescopic view means that throughout the day coaches choose to focus in and pull back to shift perspectives.

Schoolwide coaching involves looking at trends or areas of need throughout classrooms (see Table 1). For example, one might notice that students throughout the middle school are struggling with writing. That would lead to the questions, What preparation do the teachers in middle school need to help their students? What structures do the language arts teachers have in place to help students learn to write? How can the content area teachers contribute to students' writing more effectively? And, of course, what preparation can happen in the lower grades to better prepare students for the demands of middle school writing?

In our own coaching positions, we often find ourselves with a pile of papers in hand, looking at the individual essays from one class, talking with teachers about a particular technique, while simultaneously thinking about trends in instruction throughout the school building. Balancing these two views can be difficult. Sometimes, it is easy to get lost in the

Table 1. What Literacy Coaches Do Schoolwide

1. Collect and analyze writing samples
2. Develop systems for teachers to learn from one another (peer observations)
3. Set up inquiry groups (book study groups, group answering a focus question)
4. Identify schoolwide assessments/rubrics
5. Help school to determine qualities of effective literacy instruction
6. Assist grades in articulating goals for literacy
7. Administer/coordinate assessments
8. Develop/plan curriculum
9. Identify helpful resources for school to purchase
10. Establish grade-level literacy teams
11. Develop a common language around literacy
12. Identify trends or areas of need in instruction
13. Develop schoolwide structures to support literacy, portfolios
14. Organize parent literacy nights

big picture and spend time away from classrooms. Other times, our focus is too narrow and we might spend the majority of our time devoted to one grade level or teacher and not think about the implications of this particular grade's curriculum and instruction on the whole school. Finding the balance between the microscopic and macroscopic view is a balancing act that requires constant adjustment. During different points throughout the year, you will find that your role as literacy coach can lean to one side. See Figure 2 for an example of one coach's morning. Throughout her meetings with teachers and time in classrooms, she shifts between her views. Notice how in the coach's first observation of the day in one classroom, her perspective shifts from the implications of the question on one particular classroom to the implications this question has schoolwide.

Sometimes as you shift between different perspectives, teachers, and classrooms, the activities that you do as a coach may feel disjointed. On any given day, ordering books, looking at spreadsheets of student scores, and meeting with teachers can feel very disconnected. In addition, there are times when you may have to deal with issues that seemingly have no relevance to your job description or title. These tasks might include responding to a request from a teacher with issues about classroom management or general questions about curriculum

Figure 2. A Glimpse at a Literacy Coach's Schedule

A schedule of a coach's day	Coach's reflection on schoolwide and classroom perspective
8:00 a.m. Welcome students	
8:30 a.m. Observe in second-grade room—Focus question: "How do I enhance students' ability to answer inferential questions?"	Schoolwide: This question is something our school is trying to answer because the literacy team has noted that this is a problem for our students. I am spending time in a number of classrooms (K–8), observing the types of questions that students ask. Classroom: I am observing in Ms. T's second-grade room. I will meet with her tomorrow and show her the data I collected. I hope by looking at the data she will reflect on her style of questioning and begin to think about the questions she asks before she teaches the class.
9:15 a.m. Meet with sixth-grade teachers to discuss "what type of data" they would like to analyze to understand students' comprehension	Schoolwide: I wonder how teachers are determining whether a student comprehends a particular text? As a school, do we have a standard approach for this task? Would it help to have teachers share the ways they assess comprehension during professional development? Classroom: Ms. W. is very interested in helping her students comprehend more difficult texts. She has mainly used multiple-choice questions to assess student understanding. She is interested in finding other data that might shed light on student comprehension.
10:00 a.m. Meet with third-grade team to look at expository essay	Schoolwide: By developing this rubric, the third-grade team is making clear their goals for writing. Wouldn't it be helpful if each grade articulated their expectations for their students and made it accessible to all teachers, students, and parents? Classroom: The teachers are in the process of developing a student-friendly rubric that students can use to evaluate their own writing.
12:30 p.m. Review DIBELS Scores; prepare report for principal/grade-level team	Schoolwide: The data shows we have made gains in basic decoding, yet many of our students are still showing up in academic warning when it comes to fluency. What strategies can we do to help student fluency? How much does students' lack of fluency contribute to reading comprehension problems? Classroom: Ms. Z has offered to share some of her strategies for teaching students to decode with Mr. P, a new teacher. Can I set up a way so that Mr. P can observe Ms. Z during the day?

planning or time management. Effective coaches understand that literacy teaching in any school does not occur in a vacuum. Teachers and students deal with a number of issues each day that might affect how you coach and even how you organize or deliver your schoolwide professional development. The question becomes, How can you weave together the different activities so that they are focused on the goals of improving students' learning?

Student Work: The Literacy Coach's Way In

There is something powerful about looking at a piece of work done by a student. By studying the work, insights about the student as learner open in front of you. In one piece of writing, you can see a student as a reader and writer, and you can make some good guesses about the type of instruction he or she has received in writing up to that point.

Look, for example, at the piece of writing in Figure 3. What do you see in this student's writing? What do you learn about her as a writer? Do you notice how she organizes her information into paragraphs? Do you hear the writer's voice and appreciate her sincere entreaty for new shoes? Do you focus on grammar and punctuation? If she were your student, what would be your next steps?

Making sense of the work is like solving a mystery. It is filled with clues about the individual as a learner. Learning how to look at and make sense of this information and use it takes time, practice, and a trained eye. Often it is best understood in collaboration with other teachers. This is where the literacy coach comes in. Coaches can guide teachers, modeling how to make sense of formative assessments and providing leadership to create an environment of collaboration, reflection, and professional learning.

Since the arrival of No Child Left Behind, there has been a windfall of literacy assessments. There are literacy tests for every student from kindergarten through high schools that attempt to shed light on students' literacy achievement, from their ability to decode a word to their ability to write a complex analytical essay. Usually the information from these assessments are returned in the form of a number; for example, "She got a 4 on the writing test," "The class only got 50% of the vocabulary in context questions correct," and "They got 75% of the

Figure 3. Student Work Sample

Dad can you buy me some
new claths and shoes because I got
good grades on my progres report.
I got As and Bs so I should
get some new cloths and shoes.
I worked hard to get
those grades. I studyed a lot
for those good grades so please buy me some cloths
and shoes.

Dad the kind of Cloths I want
is Sandles, flip flops, dress shoes, mihes,
air force ones. Dad I want some
new shoes because I will burn up in
those Timberlins and those rocket dog shoes
Dad I want some new shoes because
Summer is coming up and I dont want
my feet to swet in Tims those
are boots and I need those for wintter.

inference type questions correct—but there were only four of them on the test." Schools are overflowing with data and up to their ears with statistics. Yet most schools and teachers stop short of using data to create a plan to improve instruction. Some are unsure of what data to use, some are stuck on how to make meaning of the data they have, and others do not know what the next steps should be after analyzing the data. This contributes to data inertia—a symptom of schoolwide paralysis where information lies untouched. While coaches may glance at the information, most often it becomes mountain-high stacks of paper, filed away in empty drawers.

Moving Beyond Test Scores to Find Formative Data

In the past, schools received their test scores, and if they were lucky, by the end of the year, they could spend time talking about how students did. The information given to them was summative; its main purpose was to evaluate how much a student knew or didn't know at the end of a predetermined time period. Teaching was rarely changed based on data; instead, the information was used to label, grade, or determine whether students should move on to the next grade and was then neatly filed away. On the other hand, formative data stay in the forefront of your mind as you are planning instruction. Formative data are discussed, analyzed, and interpreted to adjust the curriculum to suit the needs of the learners.

What is formative data? Data that were once summative become formative when teachers begin to use them to reflect on and adapt what they are doing. Formative assessments are not end-of-the-year tests; they are ongoing, often informal assessments of student knowledge. Using a formative assessment is like traveling with a GPS unit. Formative data allow you to constantly readjust, make you aware of wrong turns, and alert you to other challenges that get in your way of getting to the target.

Formative assessments are not necessarily paper-and-pencil tests. They can take the form of observational notes from a teacher, a student's homework assignment from the night before, the number of times a student raised his hand in class, a benchmark standardized test in the beginning or middle of the year, or a conference between a teacher and student about a book. Other examples of formative assessments include journal entries, running records, essays, fluency reads, developmental spelling tests, exit slips, graphic organizers, and interviews. In fact, formative data is the student work that fills schools. It overflows student folders, hangs on every bulletin board, and makes up classroom conversations. And yet somehow student work is often overlooked.

Teachers and coaches will spend hours thinking about a lesson but do not necessarily use the student work produced as a gauge of students' understanding or how successful instruction was. Instead, oftentimes a grade is given to a student and the teacher moves on to the next chapter, regardless of whether the students are with the teacher or not. For teachers to assimilate new ideas into their knowledge base, they need opportunities to pose questions, view situations from multiple perspectives, examine their personal beliefs and assumptions, and experiment with new approaches (Langer, Colton, & Goff, 2003). Coaches can help to provide the context for these conditions so that teachers can make the necessary adjustments after the analysis of the formative data. Unfortunately, it is not uncommon for many schools to wait for end-of-the-year tests to give them an understanding of how successful their instruction has been rather than to reflect regularly on what the formative data shows them. Black and Wiliam (1998) explain, "When the cook tastes the soup, that's formative assessment; when the customer tastes the soup, that's summative assessment." As coaches, we need to give back the control of the classroom to teachers. Teachers should not wait until the end of the year to find out what is effective; they should be "tasting the soup" daily, analyzing the formative work of students, and varying the recipe for students with individual needs.

How Can Coaches Use Formative Data?

How do you approach your work with teachers so that both individual coaching sessions as well as professional development workshops can remain continually focused on student progress? Even doing a wonderful demonstration lesson, conducting a workshop for the staff on a new teaching method, or meeting with a grade level to plan a lesson is important, but it is only one step in a coaching cycle. How can you connect your daily coaching activities with teachers so that each part is integrated into a process where teachers can reflect on how their own practice affects student learning?

We developed the formative analysis cycle to describe the daily process of planning and reflecting on instruction based on student work and other formative data (see Figure 4; a reproducible version of the formative data analysis cycle can be found in Appendix A so that you may easily share this as a handout with teachers). This cycle provided the backbone for our work with teachers. We used the cycle both to inform the work of our professional development workshops and our one-on-one coaching with the idea that teachers would begin to use this process independently to plan their instruction.

Figure 4. Formative Data Analysis Cycle

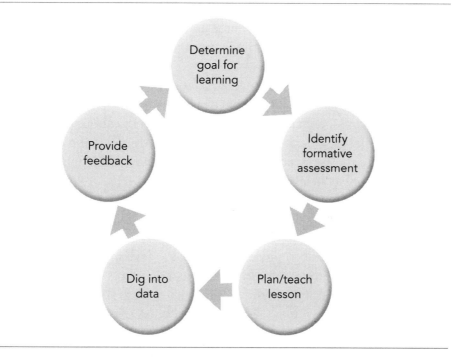

In the first phase, teachers choose a goal for student learning. But where does this goal come from? Although informed by grade-level and state standards, the goal of learning comes from the student work itself. Teachers start by looking at formative information and ask themselves, What does this data show that students need to learn? Do all students show they need to learn the same thing? The goal must be nameable, something that teachers can share with students, and influenced by grade-level standards.

As teachers move to the next step, they then ask themselves, How will I be able to recognize student understanding? How will I know if students get it? Sometimes teachers begin to plan wonderful and engaging lessons without considering how they will be able to assess student understanding. But when teachers do not identify what they will use as formative information, how can they determine their next steps for instruction? How will they know if they need to reteach or move on?

Identifying good formative assessments is challenging. This is where your coaching can play a big role as you remind teachers about the task of determining a formative assessment and suggest ways they might do so. In Chapters 2 and 3, we examine how coaches can support teachers during this phase of the cycle.

The third step is where the teachers develop and teach a lesson in the context of the formative data they have previously looked at. What do I know about the students in my class? What do I know about their learning style? How will I best be able to help them reach this learning goal? At this point of the cycle, coaches may go into a classroom to model or collaboratively teach a lesson.

During the fourth step, teachers then dig into the data to determine student understanding. Sometimes the data might just be based on classroom observation and other times it is a more formal assessment. As they look at the work, questions arise. Did I make my goals clear to my students? Was the formative assessment a good measure of student progress? As teachers look at their work, they pay careful attention to the data, jotting down notes about individuals and putting students into groups based on instructional need.

In the fifth step, teachers provide feedback to students about their progress. This feedback is differentiated based on the needs of the students. For some, it might simply be a comment or a question. Others may receive their feedback in the form of a lesson. Once again the cycle begins as teachers identify a target for learning in the context of formative data.

Take, for example, an eighth-grade teacher who looks at her state's standards and decides she must teach her students how to write a persuasive essay. She breaks down this goal into subtopics and chooses one to begin to focus on: identifying a position and supporting an argument. She moves to the second step and determines what type of data she can analyze to understand if her students can do this skill. For this, she chooses a simple position/evidence graphic organizer for students to complete. For the third step, the teacher develops and teaches a lesson on persuasion and uses the same graphic organizer to practice developing an argument together as a class. Later, students are given a different topic and asked to use the graphic organizer to plan their ideas. In the fourth step, the teacher determines the success of her instruction by looking through the students' completed graphic organizers, analyzing what students understood and what they still need to continue to practice. She makes notes for individuals and groups of students. For the fifth step, she determines how best to share their progress and set goals for the students. She decides to meet with students with similar needs in groups and show them a model of a graphic organizer where the student has provided clear support for their point of view. She begins the cycle again as she identifies new learning goals and lessons based on the student work she has analyzed.

What Is Formative Coaching?

We developed the term *formative coaching* to describe an approach to literacy coaching in which student work serves as the foundation for mentoring and professional development and provides the context for collaboration between teachers. A formative coach works with teachers individually or in a larger setting to make meaning of formative data and understand the implications on a classroom and whole-school perspective. The formative coaching cycle helped us figure out the various ways we could support teachers in their planning and instruction. It gave structure to our responsibilities and connected the time teachers had together for whole-school professional development. No longer did we give the one-shot workshop where we unloaded information on teachers and then expected them to implement these techniques. Rather, the time teachers had for professional development was integrated into a cycle of effective instruction, which encouraged them to collaborate, communicate, explore, and hold one another accountable for good teaching and, most importantly, student learning.

Rather than travel in lockstep, the needs of teachers and students would determine the phase of the cycle. In this way, our professional development became differentiated based on the needs of the adults in the community. For instance, the second-grade teachers might be developing a learning activity, the fifth grade might be analyzing an essay, special education teachers might be sharing their data with others, and the eighth grade might be looking at their standards and discussing how to make clear their goals and targets.

How Can Formative Coaching Help Me?

If you are like many coaches, you are working alone in a school, perhaps without any clear job description other than make sure students are learning. Whether you are a veteran or a newbie coach to your building, you have probably already realized the challenges of providing meaningful professional development for teachers. Using the model of formative coaching can help serve a vital role in the work you do every day with teachers, students, and administrators.

Formative coaching can

- Provide a way to develop relationships with teachers and students
- Create situations to encourage reflective classroom teaching
- Provide a context for collaboration between teachers of the same and different grade levels
- Allow you to develop a plan for your coaching

Developing Relationships

One of the most important aspects of your job is getting to know teachers and students. The success of your coaching depends on your consistent effort to build your relationships with teachers so that they begin to see you as someone who is a support rather than someone there to criticize or spy on them. The way you position yourself in your school becomes extremely important. As a literacy coach, it is assumed that you have deep knowledge of how students learn to read and write. This does not mean you have to have all the answers. In many instances, it is best to position yourself as a classroom collaborator rather than an expert. We have all known coaches who have come into classrooms as if they were the host of a makeover show: Fixing up libraries, handing out activity sheets, rearranging the desks, adding to word walls, and reworking the teachers' plans, the coach storms into one room after the other, making over the school. Though mostly the coach's suggestions are based on good intentions, the coach has not established a relationship with the teachers. The suggestions may sound like district mandates or simply arbitrary preferences. Why should teachers make changes (other than because the coach told them to do so) when they cannot see how these suggestions are connected to student learning?

Formative coaches build relationships as they look through student work with teachers. Team teaching, modeling, and coplanning are born out of an authentic need as determined by the work of the students. Formative coaches get to know teachers and learn about their instruction through the work of the students. They learn about the individual strengths and weaknesses of the class. Formative coaching is not about assigning the coach to work with a newly hired teacher who has never taught reading, the difficult teacher who dislikes collaboration, or the brand-new teacher who is fresh out of college. The idea behind formative coaching is really to support the continued progress of the students. Whether the students are high achieving or currently struggling, the coach can work collaboratively with the teacher to help the students excel in reading. While a reflective teacher may ponder many issues in isolation, their true inspiration comes from sharing both challenges and successes with their students, colleagues, and parents (Langer et al., 2003). Formative coaching helps teachers forge these relationships.

As the coach looks over the work with the teacher, together they develop a plan of action. This is the opening for coaching conversations and collaboration around instruction. Just saying, "Let's plan a writing lesson together" can be out of context and may even be interpreted by some as a way of the coach saying that she sees the teacher is struggling. But if looking at student work is a part of your school's culture, you will consistently be meeting to talk about instruction. One coach explains, "I want to plan with teachers, but I'm not sure how to go about it. Just going over to them and saying, 'Let's plan a lesson' is out of context because I might not even know what they are teaching. Using student work as the basis of our conversation allows for a natural opening to talk about teaching and planning." Sometimes, if you are coaching a teacher who is resistant or one with whom you do not quite click, having student work can be a buffer. It reminds both of you that you are there to help the students, and the work opens up conversations that the teacher might otherwise not want to have.

Some coaches have an even more challenging job since they are responsible for many different schools and only find themselves in a particular building a few times a month. Obviously, getting to know teachers can be more difficult when you are not consistently around. In those situations, it is most often the case that you can only form personal relationships with some of the staff. It is these teachers who can help pave the way for your work with other teachers and the school as a whole.

Encouraging Reflective Classroom Teaching

Focusing on student work allows teachers to become reflective as they evaluate their teaching. As you look at a fluency read with a teacher, asking him to reflect on what worked will draw him back to looking at his own practice. Successful teachers don't simply rely on solutions or techniques provided by others for making responsible and effective instructional decisions (Kolb, 1994; Schön, 1983, 1987). Instead, these teachers make judgments based on thoughtful analysis, problem solving, and reflection of their assessments (Colton & Sparks-Langer, 1993). Reflecting is not about passing judgment or assigning blame. It is about what approach works for students.

Sometimes a certain style of teaching or presenting information may work for one group of students but not another. In the not-so-distant past, it was common for teachers to take a "steam train" approach to their instruction and just keep pushing along to their end goal, whether the students were getting it or not. At the end of the semester, when the majority of the students failed the class, it was seen as the students' responsibility rather than anything the teacher could change. In this way, teachers were rendered powerless. Teachers who plan with formative data are aware of when students are falling behind. Rather than standing helplessly on the sidelines, teachers are front and center, asking themselves and others what they can do to make their instruction more effective. They reflect on what can they learn about their students, and they ask themselves what they can do to make sure students reach this goal. Formal and informal reflection becomes innate to teachers as they measure the effectiveness of their teaching for individuals and groups of students.

Creating a Context for Collaboration and Collegiality

Student work can create an authentic way for teachers to work collaboratively through all phases of the cycle. During grade-level meetings or professional development workshops, teachers can work together to coach one another through all phases of the cycle. Teachers begin to develop a relationship with other adult learners that is built on trust and a common goal of increased student achievement.

For instance, when we first began to use formative information to understand student reading and writing as a school, it became clear to the staff that we lacked common grade or schoolwide assessments. As teachers discussed students' reading and writing, they noticed that their language to describe what they saw was not consistent. Despite state standards, what students were supposed to accomplish by each grade level was unclear. No wonder our students were not gaining ground year after year: Our school lacked instructional coherence. One teacher might expect students to write in paragraphs, while another was fine without them. One teacher wanted students to write their personal opinions, while another teacher focused more on grammar and spelling. Who was right or wrong did not matter; as we flipped through the students' writing, we decided that improving students' literacy would be a schoolwide effort.

After determining a common assessment (running records) and a common vocabulary to discuss how students were reading, we created a display of student reading levels and asked teachers to look at the work. Teachers eagerly began to look not only at their current students but at the students they had had many years ago. It wasn't surprising that a second-grade teacher, after looking at the third-grade data, asked if perhaps the teacher of the third-grade class wanted to send her some of the struggling third graders to work at her phonics-based center. It was clear: Teachers were beginning to see the importance of each teacher's contribution in helping to educate our students. The doors of the classroom had begun to swing wide open.

Creating a Plan of Action for the Literacy Coach

As a coach, you may find yourself in a situation where you are pulled in many directions: There is the new teacher to help, the more experienced teacher who has children endlessly copying from the board, the enthusiastic teacher in kindergarten who wants to meet with you, the group of fifth-grade teachers who aren't quite sure what to teach, the fourth-grade teacher who has identified children she thinks may require special education resources, and the sixth-grade teacher who creates wonderful lessons and is just looking for some acknowledgment. How do you know where to begin? You can use formative data to help determine where you start coaching.

As you look through formative data, you can see the areas of need. Most principals do not have time to look over various student work from different grade levels in the school; instead their focus will go to test scores. However, test scores are most useful when they are springboards for discussions about curriculum and instruction. For example, when we looked at our school's test scores, we asked the question, What data can we use throughout the year as a formative assessment of students' comprehension? As a school, we determined to assess students' reading through running records. These one-on-one assessments allowed teachers to understand students' individual needs. As coaches, we were then able to look through the assessments of the students with teachers and collaborate with them on what lessons students might need.

As you begin to look at data (test or otherwise), you can see areas of need throughout the school and then rank the importance of each. This will allow you to plot a road map for your coaching and professional development. If you are not sure where to begin, take a look at the various types of formative data around you. What do you notice about it? Starting by looking at the student work will allow you to begin a conversation about curriculum and instruction.

Taking Stock

Perhaps one of the most important variables in determining your success with formative coaching is your own comfort with looking at and analyzing formative assessments. While there are no simple formulas you can apply to a running record or an essay to figure out what the students' challenges are, there are techniques to help you understand what you see and plan for instruction. Throughout this book, we provide techniques of looking at and making sense of student work. While we show examples from students, we suggest that you begin to collect student work at your own school. Keep these pieces available so that you can practice making sense of work and provide examples for your colleagues. It will most likely be you who will propel this movement throughout the school, so it is important to be enthusiastic and flexible about this process and have examples on hand to demonstrate to others.

As the coach, you certainly do not need to have all the answers; however, you should feel confident about the usefulness of examining student work and the idea that working collaboratively to understand it will help you meet students' needs.

REFLECTING AND EXTENDING

This chapter focused on the various roles coaches play in schools and how these separate activities can be linked through the process of looking at and analyzing student work. In addition, it explored the many separate tasks that coaches must do and how best to prepare yourself for the many challenges you will face as a coach.

Also in this chapter, we presented the formative data analysis cycle for analyzing student work, which presents a context for coaches to develop relationships with teachers, create situations where staff can work collaboratively with one another, as well as offer a way to design an integrated system of professional development that encourages reflective teaching. In the next chapters, we explore the process of formative coaching, beginning from data investigation to working with teachers individually and planning professional development for whole-school workshops. No matter what program, textbook, or philosophy your school supports, we show you techniques to ground your coaching in concrete data—whether it is student writing, students' verbal responses, or test scores—in order to produce student achievement.

QUESTIONS TO CONSIDER

1. What do you consider to be some of the most important tasks of a coach? Which tasks do you think are key parts of your role as a coach, and which tasks do you feel are outside of the domain of a coach? Use the Exploring Your Role as Coach form in Appendix A to jot down your ideas. Do you think the principal of your school would agree with you?

2. Think about how you spend your day. In what type of schoolwide tasks do you participate?

3. What does a collaborative school environment mean to you? Have you worked in one before?

4. Think for a moment about which coaching tasks are a concern for you. What steps can you take to prepare yourself?

5. How do you feel about formative data? How does the data play a role in your own teaching?

6. What strengths will you bring as a literacy leader? What areas are a cause for concern for you in terms of providing leadership?

CHAPTER 2

Stepping Onto the Playing Field

Imagine This!

It is the first day of school. Although the morning is going to be a busy one for all, the assistant principal wants to meet with you about forming a calendar for scheduling professional development throughout the year. He has also asked you to check in on the new fourth-grade teacher and the veteran eighth-grade teacher and to discuss with the staff the common grade-level meeting time that the district has mandated in all schools. It is important, he explains, to make sure teachers are aware of the newly revised grade-level standards now only accessible online.

Then, of course, there are the administrative tasks that you need to attend to: the shipments of books that have arrived a month later than they were expected and need to be sorted, accounted for, and then delivered to the correct people as soon as humanly possible because some teachers have no books. A report is also needed on which teachers have working computers in the classroom and also, the assistant principal adds, on the number of teachers that have classroom libraries. As you take notes, your list grows.

Weeks go by, and you diligently check off items on your list. You are so busy that you haven't even had time to meet all the teachers, let alone go on any classroom visits. Your first free morning, you walk through the hallways, looking for an open classroom door that you can just pop your head into so you can start looking at literacy instruction. But all the doors are closed. Where should you begin, you think? Is it acceptable to just walk in and start observing a teacher? You are pretty sure some of the teachers are not even sure who you are. Should you schedule a time to meet with grade levels and introduce yourself? You think quietly to yourself, Where do I begin? You find yourself poised outside of a closed door, not sure if you should open it.

You may wonder why a whole chapter should be devoted to stepping onto the playing field of literacy coaching and getting to know the team in your school. Shouldn't it be the case that teachers will want to work with you given that you are trying to help their students succeed? Won't they be able to see your good intentions? In fact, for many coaches, getting to know teachers is one of the most challenging aspects of the position.

While you may have been hired as the coach of your school, it isn't until school opens that you truly begin trying out for your position. You may be called a literacy coach from the start, but each day you will need to prove your worth to teachers and demonstrate how you are an asset to them and your school. For most schools, the role of literacy coach is relatively new. Even if teachers have interacted with literacy coaches before, the characteristics and responsibilities of the position vary from school to school and are still being defined. Teachers and principals are sometimes unsure of what to expect from a literacy coach. Will you be in your office looking at test scores, meeting with groups of high-needs students, or visiting and team teaching in classrooms? For some teachers, especially before they get to know a literacy coach, there may be an inherent mistrust of someone dropping in on the classroom. In their mind, you might be an interloper and perhaps a spy for the administration. Your position may elicit bitterness from other teachers because you are not in charge of students all day. From their perspective, it may seem that you get to tell teachers what to do and do not have the responsibility of working in a classroom. It is during this initial phase that you must prove that, above all, you are a teacher, learner, and reflective practitioner who is committed to the students.

In this chapter, we offer suggestions on how to build relationships with teachers and ways to begin to understand the needs of your school by learning about the formative and summative data in your school. These two steps will help you prepare for the more intricate work of formative coaching as you establish a game plan and specific strategies for helping individual teachers. On the outside, these steps are simple, yet add in the other myriad responsibilities coaches have, and it is no wonder why they are often overlooked.

Step 1: Building Relationships

As you begin formative coaching, you will need to find your way into classrooms. In some cases, you may be directed to work with a grade level or individual teachers, while in other coaching positions, the decision will be left up to you. School improvement is a process that is accomplished teacher by teacher. It is often the case that we have felt our coaching was the most meaningful when it has been one-on-one, toiling side by side with the teacher during a lesson, or sitting during a free period to plan out ideas. But how do you get to the point where you spend a good part of your coaching time interacting with teachers and students? While jumping right in works for some, most people need a plan. How can you open the doors of the classrooms so that teachers can begin to see you as a resource?

Knowles (1990) describes the following six characteristics of adult learners:

1. Desire to know: Adults are pragmatic. They want to know the goal of the learning situation and why it's important.

2. Self-concept: Adult learners are self-directed and often do not want to relinquish control to others.

3. Experience: Adults rely on experience to draw upon in their decision making.

4. Readiness to learn. Adults are able to see the relevance of what they are learning for application in their real life.

5. Orientation to learning. Adults want to learn skills that are practical to their own life and may not be interested in underlying theories.

6. Motivation to learn: Adults are responsive to external motivations (salary, incentives) but also are internally motivated. (pp. 57–63)

With these six characteristics in mind, coaches can begin to plan a course of action to work with teachers in their classrooms that will maximize their effectiveness as a coach. Formative data and looking at student work can serve as the building block that supports the six characteristics of the adult learner (see Figure 5). There is no better way of making the time you spend with teachers meaningful than showing them how this can translate into student success. The usefulness of a particular

Figure 5. Student Work and the Connection to Characteristics of Adult Learners

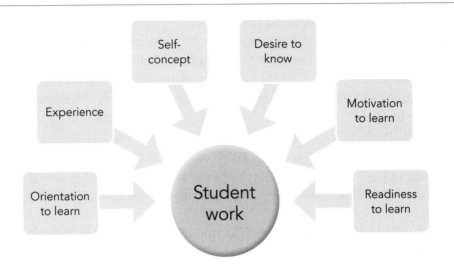

teaching technique speaks for itself when teachers see their students improving. In many schools, data become punitive as teachers receive accolades or condemnation based on student improvement in reading scores. But through a different lens, data can be empowering, allowing teachers to have insight into what their students know and how they learn.

The job-embedded part of coaching that takes you into teachers' classrooms to work with them is perhaps the most important part of the position because it allows teachers to understand, observe, and partake in teaching techniques in the context of their classroom and the students that they know. It is also one method of building relationships with teachers as you both share your thinking and take risks trying out new types of instruction.

Meeting the Team

One of the most crucial aspects of coaching is the relationships you will form with the adults in your building. Some of these relationships will be closer and more comfortable than others. Although walking into some classrooms and talking to the teachers will feel as comfortable as planning with a good friend, other rooms may be more intimidating and require a few deep breaths before even entering. In both of these instances, these professional relationships will take effort and monitoring. Sometimes, it can feel more uncomfortable asking the classroom teacher with whom you grab drinks after work to reflect on her teaching than the teacher with whom you do not have a personal rapport. Both of these relationships require openness, trust, professionalism, and an understanding of your role as coach.

Getting to know the teachers at your school will require creating opportunities where you can learn about them both as educators and people. In the leadership position of a coach, it will often be your responsibility to communicate with the staff and administration about issues pertaining to literacy both in small and large groups. Managing relationships with the staff means knowing when to offer to model a lesson in a classroom, when to push a team to reflect on their curriculum and instruction, when to be a sounding block for teaching ideas, and when simply to be a support and to listen.

Making Introductions

Whether you are new to your school or a returning coach, the beginning of the year is a good time to make introductions. Even before the year has begun, many coaches send out a note to teachers introducing themselves and the role they hope to provide. Some coaches make a packet of helpful resources to give to teachers. In our school, we compile a list of curriculum resources (our literacy vision, helpful graphic organizers, assessments that we use, sight word lists) for new and returning teachers. Figure 6 is an example of what goes into our school literacy pack. We find it helpful as an overview for new teachers about the vision of literacy instruction in our school. It can serve as talking points during our initial meetings with new staff. Although we know that most teachers will not have the time to look through it right away, we go back to this binder of resources and add to it throughout the year. We always attach a note to our literacy packet, briefly introducing ourselves and giving an overview of our literacy goals for the year (see Figure 7). However, we do not make this introductory note too long or detailed because we know that at the beginning of the year most teachers do not have the time or patience to concentrate on a long memo from the literacy coach.

Figure 6. Contents Listing for Packet of Helpful Resources for Teachers

Contents
Part 1: Balanced literacy framework

1. Welcome to literacy
2. Vision and philosophy of literacy
3. Norms of professional learning community
4. Focus on instruction coherence
5. Sample schedule
6. Writing fundamentals
7. Lesson planner
8. Running records (example and coding)
9. Individual running record chart
10. Reading-level correlation chart
11. Sight word lists
12. Fluency targets by grade level
13. Helpful websites

Figure 7. Introductory Letter to Teachers

Dear Teachers:

Welcome to literacy. How time flies! This is our third year of balanced literacy as a school, and with each year, our professional learning community strengthens the model and identifies effective teaching strategies.

Last school year, we began to examine how to further build coherence in literacy instruction. As a school, we chose to incorporate the teaching of six essential reading strategies (based on those from Stephanie Harvey's *Strategies That Work*) to teach throughout each grade at NTA. We will continue to explore how to use these strategies both in the classroom and during grade-level meetings.

The summer was filled with hard work. In an effort to further build coherence, grade levels met to further hone end-of-year target statements and assessments. In the spirit of collaboration, grade levels identified "end-of-year targets" and "grade-level sight words" and assessments, so that each grade level could build upon the work of the previous year.

This year, we will continue to focus on the analysis of formative assessments (student work). We will devote time during professional development, grade-level meetings, and individual coaching meetings to analyzing a variety of formative data to help inform instruction and build coherence throughout the building.

The adventure continues. Hold on tight—this promises to be quite a ride!

Gabrielle & Maya

We have found that, although our initial note is important, sending group or individualized follow-up notes throughout the year is a good way of offering continued support and that later in the year teachers may be more open and know specifically the type of support they need.

Stepping Out

In the beginning of the year, it is also a good time to personally check in with teachers. Sometimes, you may be able to schedule formal meetings, and other times, it may rely on just stopping by for five minutes or sending them a personal note.

During these informal meetings, your role is to listen and identify areas that you might be able to support them in with your coaching (see Figure 8). We always ask the teachers if the time we have chosen to drop by is convenient, and we do not expect them to stop organizing their books or hanging up their bulletin board simply because we dropped in. In fact, when we can, we help. During this time we may ask the teachers general questions about their classroom or their students. We call this method a "quickstop." It's a fast and efficient way to build relationships with teachers

Figure 8. Informal Meeting Between Teacher and Coach

in an informal setting. Sometimes the informal settings are where you might be able to get the most feedback from teachers to support formative coaching. Some general quickstop questions you might consider are as follows:

- Do you have all the books you need to get started? Is there anything you have been looking for that you can't find?
- What are you looking forward to teaching this year?
- What are you noticing about the students this year? Is there anyone that stands out to you right away?

These quickstop meetings can serve as the initial springboard for more in-depth meetings later. They are also often a way to get to know teachers and to begin to build relationships with them. During these times, we also reiterate that coaches are there to support teachers and that during the first few weeks we want to arrange a few minutes during the day to introduce ourselves to students. This lets teachers know that the focus for everyone involved is on student learning. We have found that after introducing ourselves to the class, it naturally leads to later conversations about the students in the class. You might notice a particular student in the class and then inquire about him or her. Learning about the students is an important pathway to talking about curriculum and instruction.

As you meet the students, you should make an effort to get to know them by name. One trick to help you do this is to ask the office for class rosters. As you begin to learn about the students, jot down quick notes about their learning characteristics or styles. During a free moment, you can casually ask teachers about these students. Most teachers love talking about the colorful personalities in their class.

Stepping out involves taking risks. It means offering to help teachers in their classrooms and getting to know them as people. This can be as simple as providing assistance hanging up a bulletin board or helping them set up their classroom. Following through and checking in with teachers on a regular basis is an important part of relationship building. The e-mail in Figure 9 provides an example of a follow-up that was sent after an informal conversation with a teacher. The suggestions are focused and short—something the teacher could implement with or without your

Figure 9. Example of Follow-Up E-Mail Sent After Informal Meeting With Teacher

To: MsT@teacher.com

From: literacycoach@teacher.com

Re: A thought about organizing

Ms. T,

I just wanted to let you know that I enjoyed setting up the bulletin board with you yesterday. The students seemed to have a fun time writing about their imaginary trips. You mentioned during our conversation that John had problems organizing his research. Have you thought about using index cards to help him organize his work? If not, this is a suggestion that might be useful for him and has worked well for me in the past with students. This allows for a "tactile" approach for organization. I'd be happy to talk more about this or come into your classroom and work with John on this.

Best,

Your literacy coach

help. The literacy coach has opened the door for conversation and offered a concrete suggestion that could be modeled for the teacher.

It is important to note that many of your initial interactions with teachers may not be formal coaching conversations. Offering assistance with mundane tasks may provide a moment for a discussion on instruction. As teachers begin to see that you can be a resource rather than a nuisance, they will begin to seek your help.

Surveying teachers with a needs-assessment form is a good way of having them identify what type of help they would like. However, if you give out a needs assessment before you begin to know the teachers, it is likely that you may not know what questions to ask and you will not get much of a response. Part of teachers feeling comfortable asking for your help involves them trusting you. They may be worried that if they identify certain needs, that this information will be relayed to the principal. If possible, establish a rapport first with teachers and then begin to survey them.

Literacy Gatherings

One way of opening classroom doors is by creating a regular time and place for teachers to get together and talk about literacy and instruction.

For example, a former principal for a public school in New York ended every week with a weekly morning gathering called "Toasty Fridays." Before class, teachers gathered together to eat toast and jam (he provided both) and talk about nothing in particular. Although the meetings were informal, teachers often ended up talking about students, ways they could collaborate, or teaching ideas. Toasty Fridays provided an opportunity for teachers to get to know one another.

Often, I would use these Friday meetings to have coaching conversations or set up times to visit classrooms. Building on this idea, as a literacy coach, you might decide to host a weekly or monthly breakfast to talk about topics pertaining to literacy (see Figure 10). Determine whether you want your meeting to be a formal book group or a more informal gathering. Choose a focus for the meeting and then decide how structured you want the gathering to feel. Consider the following planning guide when thinking about a literacy meeting:

Figure 10. Literacy Gathering

- What is the goal of the literacy meetings? How will you measure your progress toward this goal?
- What kind of topics do you want to discuss with this group?
- How often do you want to meet? How much time will you have? Where will you meet?
- How many teachers do you think will attend? How can you recruit others?
- How will you spread the word about your meeting? Do you need to get the principal's permission?
- What is the incentive for teachers to come to this meeting?
- Do you want teachers to casually talk or will you take a more structured approach to sharing the information?
- Will you be the one leading the meeting or can you recruit a teacher to do this?

Some coaches prefer a more structured book group where a certain resource or strategy is discussed. Others may choose a more informal gathering where conversation is free-flowing about a particular topic. What type of meetings will work for your school? Consider the following literacy breakfast meetings:

- Lesson share: Strategy/best lesson share
- Story shares: Discussions about children's literature
- Teachers as writers: Teachers share their own writing
- The one that won't get away: A sustained focus on a particular student or group of students throughout the year
- Show and tell: Gathering of teachers to show compelling research articles or books and tell how they have used the information in their classroom

In all styles of gathering, the meetings will provide an opportunity for teachers to get to know one another and, ultimately, build the professional learning community of your school. Developing a community of teachers who are knowledgeable and focused on literacy will propel school change. Part of the job of a literacy coach is to provide teachers with opportunities to get to know one another as educators and as people. In the past, we have also used a literacy newsletter and a website that highlighted what teachers were working on in their classrooms and that featured a column with a get-to-know-you section about one specific teacher. You would not believe how excited a group of adults could be over whose picture and story would be chosen for the monthly newsletter. In Chapter 6, we will delve into the process of affecting whole-school change, but as you think about how to work with teachers one on one, begin to reflect on how your individual coaching will create a space for systemic reform throughout the school.

Most of all, make time to leave your office and be available to plan, analyze student work, or visit classrooms as necessary. Depending on the nature of your school, you may be tasked with work that brings you away from the classroom and into your office. Analyzing summative data and developing professional development are important parts of many coaching jobs, but they should not overshadow the time you spend in classrooms working with teachers. Even in cases where your time is scarce, block out a period during the week where you are available to meet the myriad demands that might arise based on the needs of the teachers. See Table 2 for a list of tips for opening classroom doors—and keeping them open.

Resistance Training

While most teachers will be open to working collaboratively with a coach, each individual in the school will be on a different continuum of development, and all teachers must be respected equally as professionals. As a coach, some of the best staff development you will receive will be from the teachers in your school. While some will encourage you as you practice and develop the art of coaching, others may not be as willing to be part of your vision of coaching.

No book on literacy coaching would be complete without spending some time preparing coaches to deal with resistant teachers. In every school, no matter how supportive of a coach you are, there will be those who challenge you, sometimes openly and sometimes more discreetly. Most resistance is due to fear of change. Even though you may see your role as a support to teachers, inherently literacy coaching is about change. You may be hoping to develop a professional learning community within your school, help teachers become more reflective about their instruction,

Table 2. Steps for Opening the Door and Keeping It Open

Five steps for opening the door
1. Ask the teacher for permission to visit the classroom to meet students and introduce yourself.
2. Know students by name.
3. Eat lunch with the teachers and follow up on informal conversations about students.
4. Develop a literacy newsletter and solicit teacher help or feature a teacher and his or her students.
5. Host a Friday literacy breakfast where you feature resources.

Five steps to keeping the door open
1. Offer to help in the classroom with a group of students.
2. Look at student work on the walls and in folders, and ask questions about the work you see.
3. Offer to track student work and collect data based on questions or concerns that the teacher has expressed.
4. Ask the teacher what resources or materials are needed to support lessons and discuss the materials and follow up about their effectiveness.
5. Develop a needs assessment from the teacher about the type of assistance they need and the frequency desired.

or even simply to set up a system where students' portfolios of work can follow them through the grade levels. No matter how minor the idea seems to you, it involves change. And many teachers are wary of change. These challenges provide coaches with meaningful opportunities to develop their listening and empathy skills. For instance, new teachers may have been taught one way of teaching and then told, only a few years later, that this method was wrong, so keep this in mind if you encounter resistance from those who are relatively new to teaching. For some, school change during their teaching career has been defined by the show they have to put on whenever a district official makes the rounds visiting their school. If you have taught for more than a few years, you likely have also felt the swing of the pendulum and been told to toss out instructional techniques and curriculum that you may have considered worthwhile.

Consider now the position of literacy coach from a teacher's perspective. Imagine what you might ask if you were a teacher at your school.

> Who exactly is the coach. and what is her intention? Is she just the mouthpiece for the district, mindlessly promoting the newest teaching

technique? Has she really considered the implications of the changes and how they will affect teachers? Is she being realistic about implementation? Is she being considerate of my time?

Usually, when we meet resistance we are filled with an overwhelming impulse for either flight or fight, depending upon the situation and our proclivity for dealing with confrontation. Yet as a coach, you will have to override both these instincts. In 600 BCE, Lao-Tzu explained that in the face of resistance people should be like water. He explained, "Water is fluid, soft, and yielding. But water will wear away rock." We like the metaphor of water because it encapsulates the rushing movement and the fluid and reflective nature of coaching. Sometimes, as a coach, we can sweep others up with us, capturing them in the momentum. Others times, we will encounter resistance. Though we wrap around impediments, we remain persistent in our path, with the hope that, over time, the resistance will begin to yield or a new better path will emerge (see Table 3 for suggestions on ways to handle resistance).

In fact, it has often been the case that the teachers that were the most resistant have inspired us to be more reflective of our own coaching. It is they who have made us look deeper into our ideas and beliefs. And it is they who made us realize the importance of using formative data when discussing instruction. With the most resistant teachers, looking at data can be a safe way to talk about teaching. The data serve as springboard for conversations and allows for both coach and teacher to be more focused on student needs rather than on each other's personalities.

Table 3. Ways to Handle Resistance

- See the value in those that challenge you to dig deeper.
- Give yourself a break.
- Do not take resistance personally.
- Realize that you don't need an answer for every question.
- Know what is in your domain to change and what is not.
- Establish personal boundaries and think about how you will handle situation if these boundaries are crossed.

Facing Your Fears

Developing relationships with teachers in your school can be challenging. As the school's literacy coach, teachers throughout the school will know your name and have opinions about you, notice with whom you meet, and discuss what suggestions you may have. And although there are teachers who may approach you for help, more often it is the case that you will have to seek them out, repeatedly and consistently, until a professional relationship is formed and they begin to value the professional relationship you have. In one word, literacy coaching takes chutzpah.

While there are many people who say they are too scared to step inside a classroom to teach students, to be honest, there is nothing more frightening than stepping inside a school classroom in front of critical adults who may expect you to be an expert in all areas of literacy and teaching and who may notice any of your failures. It is clear that teaching adults poses a whole new set of challenges, most of which literacy coaches are never trained to handle.

Remember, coaching is not a job for wallflowers. It is not about blending into the background or just having an in-depth knowledge of literacy. It is a leadership position that will test your teaching skills and your abilities to work and collaborate with individuals and groups. Some teachers will be open to your role and appreciate your help, while others might be more reluctant and sometimes even openly defiant. Working effectively with teachers means knowing yourself and recognizing your own strengths and weaknesses. Once you are open about your fears, you can begin to work on how to ameliorate the situation.

Take, for example, when Gabrielle, one of the authors of this book, was asked in her first coaching job in New York City to work with a kindergarten teacher who was not receptive. To make matters worse, Gabrielle had never taught children that young, and she was worried that her lack of experience would make her an easy target for teachers to dismiss. She quickly ran to the library and read as many books as she could find on early literacy and spent time observing students and children. Gabrielle did not advertise her lack of kindergarten or coaching experience, but she knew that the teachers, just like students, might smell "fresh blood."

The first to confront her was a veteran teacher who often scowled and was known for her sarcastic comments during every staff meeting. She stopped Gabrielle on one of her coffee breaks and started to question her experience. Where had she taught? What grades? Finally, she looked Gabrielle in the eye and in a raspy voice asked, "How did you get an out-of-the classroom job? That's the job they give to teachers as a reward for teaching for 30 years. Who did you know to get that?" She took one more sip of her coffee and added in a raspy voice, "Honey, no one is going to ever listen to you. You don't look old enough to know anything." Gabrielle felt herself go pale but stammered something like, "We'll see," and quickly ran away from her. Her heart was pounding, mainly because the teacher had articulated many of the fears that Gabrielle had had swirling around in her own head. And, subconsciously, Gabrielle knew that many teachers, though they smiled politely, probably had the same questions. At the time, Gabrielle had no answers for the teacher's questions. How would she have a discussion about teaching with a person who had been teaching longer than she had? How could she talk about improving literacy for a grade she had never taught?

The truth is that no matter how long you have been a literacy coach or how many years of experience you have had as a classroom teacher, there will be a fear associated with being a mentor or a coach to other teachers. As a literacy coach, you know that you are supposed to be a model for literacy instruction. And though you may feel positive about your skills, everyone faces some anxiety about their own ability to do the job. Perhaps you are concerned about your ability to model a lesson successfully, or maybe you never felt fully competent in teaching writing to your own students. Maybe you are concerned about how to interact with veteran teachers or your principal who never seems to have time to schedule a meeting. Coaching anxieties, although different in shape and scope, are shared by everyone. The good news is that you are not alone in feeling insecure or inadequate.

Although literacy coaches should be well versed and knowledgeable about teaching reading and writing, expertise does not always engender personal confidence, and it is humanly impossible to feel confident in every area of literacy or instruction. Most likely, you will be working with teachers in grades that you yourself have never taught. Some will be more experienced than you are or excel in areas where you do not. This can all add to feelings of inadequacy. Table 4 outlines some of the fears we've experienced during our careers. Have you had any of these common feelings?

Table 4. Common Fears

- Teachers will not listen to what I have to say.
- I am not an expert in _____ and teachers will realize this.
- I am not sure how to approach my principal with new ideas.
- I have not taught ___ grade and I am supposed to mentor others.
- Even though I am telling teachers to use this, I have never tried _____ in my classroom.
- I am not confident that I can teach every child to read.
- I do not know how to work with children with learning disabilities.
- I am worried that the students will not listen to me.
- I am intimidated because I have only taught for ____ years.
- I might model a lesson that is not well received by students.

As we began the process of formative coaching, we came to realize that the key to moving our school toward improved academic achievement was to help teachers think reflectively about their students' work. The opportunity to help teachers engage in this reflection also helped to strengthen our own leadership capacity.

Once we began to be open about our fears, we started to address them head on and build our leadership capacity. This included networking with other literacy coaches, reading books about literacy coaching, and building on our own individual strengths. Some of the questions teachers confront you with may be of valid concern and important for you to address before you begin your role as literacy coach. However, most of the confrontations you will face are little more than tests—just like the ones your students gave you on your first day of school. How many times have you thought of the perfect response an hour after the situation? Having thought through and run through your responses will leave you feeling less off your guard. And in fact, there are steps you can take to better prepare yourself for your literacy coaching position. Table 5 presents some common challenges that we faced and that you might encounter as well, along with suggested responses to those challenges.

Being prepared also means taking a self-inventory of areas where you might need more professional development as a coach. Toll (2008) suggests that coaches use a tape recorder during their conferences with teachers to consider their effectiveness as a coach. While initially it may seem a bit

Table 5. Common Challenges and Sample Responses

Challenge	Response example
Why should I listen to you? You have never taught _____ grade.	This is a valid concern. You probably haven't taught every grade you will be asked to mentor. Point out the similarities between grade levels and the unique perspective that you have from your vantage point. Prepare yourself before beginning coaching. Gain as much experience with children of a variety of ages. Once you're coaching, choose a grade you are less familiar with and ask the teacher if you can work with a group of students on a regular basis. Once you have gotten to know them and tried out some of your literacy techniques, it is more likely that the teacher will be ready to listen and work with you.
Did you ever try this in your own classroom?	If the answer is no, be honest with the teacher. Point out why you think it is important to try this type of instruction. What do you believe the benefits will be? What are the challenges? Then, offer to try this in their classroom over a period of time and you can both see for yourselves the effects of a certain type of instruction.
I have been teaching this way for 15 years and it is working. Schools are always coming up with something new and then they change. I will keep doing what works for me.	What do you do in your classroom that works? Can you show me? Would you be willing to share with others? How do you measure what works in your classroom?

uncomfortable, finding a teacher who you trust and who is willing to have the conversation recorded can be an excellent way to inventory your own strengths and weaknesses as a coach.

According to Dole (2004), one of the most important aspects of literacy coaching is a deep understanding of how to teach reading and writing. If you feel you are lacking expertise in a certain area, then go seek out the information. Sign up for classes, attend workshops, work in classrooms with students, and become more knowledgeable. Knowing and understanding instruction is integral to your success as a literacy coach. As you build more confidence in your abilities, you will be more comfortable reaching out to teachers to establish meaningful relationships.

Checking In With the Captain of the Team

One of the most important relationships you will have is with your principal. The position of the school principal has transformed over time to be that of an instructional leader. Though your administrator may not know everything about curriculum, he or she must be able to make informed decisions and lead the school to ensure that quality instruction is taking place. The quality of your relationship with your school administrator can often determine how effective you can be in your position.

Before the year begins, meet with your principal and talk about the expectations of your role and the percentage of your time that he or she wants you to spend with these tasks (see Figure 11). Being clear from the start will prevent ambiguity, which leads to confusion and unclear expectations.

Questions to ask to clarify expectations of your position are as follows:

- What do you see as my role?
- What kind of everyday tasks do you see me participating in?
- How do you want to communicate? How often?

Figure 11. Meeting With the Principal

- What are your goals for literacy? How will you measure progress toward these goals? How do you see me assisting in meeting these goals?
- What type of leadership activities would you see me coordinating for professional development?
- What type of community, family, or schoolwide activities would you see me coordinating?
- How will my progress as a coach be assessed? Who do you think can be a resource for me?

Remember, you can and should suggest ideas about what you would like to do to affect literacy change. Perhaps one of the most important questions to ask your administrator is how he or she prefers to communicate with you. While we feel there is no substitute for in-person meetings, some information can be more efficiently shared through an e-mail or a note in their mailbox. One coach we know would e-mail a weekly summary of her work so that the principal would know with whom the coach was working. If possible, try and schedule a regular meeting with your principal to talk about literacy. Having or sending an agenda for the meeting will help keep discussions on target and shows the principal that you value his or her time as well as your own.

Of course, the question that begs to be asked is, What if you and your principal have different ideas about your role or what quality literacy instruction looks like? The first steps are to focus on what you share in common and to learn more about the principal's vision for the school; this will begin the conversation about teaching and learning at the school. Sometimes it can be very helpful to visit classrooms with the administrator to discuss the instruction you see. Second, talking about formative data (not only test scores) can also be a way of getting to know your principal. Appendix A offers a reproducible form you can use to reflect on the relationships you have with teachers, your principal, and the staff in your school.

Step 2: Learning About the Data in Your School

At the same time as you are beginning to get to know the teachers in your school, it is important to ask questions about the data available in your school. If your school is like most, then you will have an abundance of data at your fingertips. In fact, you might say that schools are on data overload. The statistics on everything from attendance to test scores to the number of ice cream sandwiches ordered by the cafeteria for dessert are accounted for, stored, and then reported. Yet that is often where the process ends. DuFour (2004) explains that schools suffer from being "data rich and information poor," or the DRIP syndrome. The difficulty schools have is knowing what to do with the data, what data are important, what should be closely monitored, and what decisions you should make based on the numbers.

Give Me the Stats

As a literacy coach, you may be surprised at how familiar you need to become with numbers. You may have become a reading coach because of your love for words, but you will soon see how important understanding numbers can be. In fact, if you happen to be looking for a few extra credits, we recommend taking a general research class that gives an overview of qualitative and quantitative data. In truth, most schools do not have teachers who understand how to make sense of descriptive or statistical data. If you do not trust your own skills, see if there are any researchers at local universities who are willing to help you understand what the numbers say.

The term *data mining* is often a term reserved for businesses to describe the process of making meaning out of the numbers they receive about their products. They may look at specific statistics, run a pilot group to try a new project, look for correlations, and then come to conclusions about how to create the best-selling product. Likewise, data mining can be meaningfully applied to education since the focus of analyzing data from different perspectives is to parse it into useful chunks of information. We like the term *data mining* in particular, perhaps, because of the image it brings up in our minds: a literacy coach tunneling through a large solid mountain with a small little chisel, trying to find the useful nuggets of information, observing them from different perspectives, so that she can understand what these data say about teaching and learning in her school. So often we get attached to the idea that data are numbers or percentages. But remember, formative data are also the talk, lessons, and work of teachers and students. It is the work of the literacy coach to chisel away at this information, spin it around to gain perspective, and then help teachers and administrators formulate a plan of action.

We have found it helpful to distinguish between two types of data in our discussions with teachers: (1) at-a-glance formative assessments and (2) deep-level data. At-a-glance data are quick measures that teachers use for immediate feedback about student understanding. This could be a show of hands, a thumb up or down, or a students' response to a question said in class. The formative information is usually immediate and not often stored or held on to. Sometimes, this type of data is referred to as "dip sticking" or "taking the temperature" of the class. Due to the immediacy of the feedback, this information can be very influential in determining the next steps of the teacher.

Deep-level data, on the other hand, are formative and require further analysis, or digging deeper, to be useful. For example, a student essay or response to a short-answer question can be very telling about a student's understanding but will require a further level of analysis to truly be useful (see Table 6 for a comparison of the two different types of data). At-a-glance data can be turned into deep-level data when the information is collected and analyzed at a later time. For example, a teacher might look at the number of students who raised their hand to ask a question as at-a-glance formative information and then return later to this very same data and begin to analyze who raised their hand and what they said. In another example, a teacher used a chart of students' reading levels from fall to winter as deep-level data for teachers, parents, and students (see Figure 12). Both types of data are extremely important to good teaching and will be a part of your coaching.

Table 6. At-a-Glance Data vs. Deep-Level Data

Examples of at-a-glance data	Examples of deep-level data
• Students give a thumbs up or down to show understanding • Verbal answer to a question • Number of students responding • Exit slip • Listening to a student read a book	• Running records • Essays/written responses • Fluency reads • Developmental spelling lists • Standardized test data

Figure 12. Example of Deep-Level Data

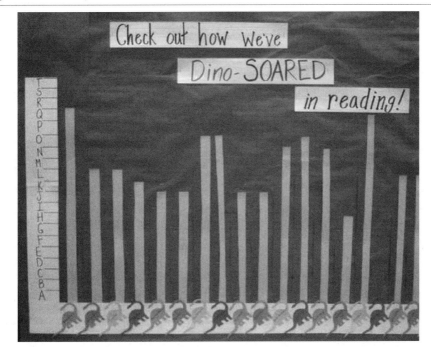

What Should I Know About Data and How Will They Influence My Coaching?

As you familiarize yourself with your school, make it a priority to find out what types of standardized data are available to you. Are there reading tests that show the types of questions students struggled with the most in a particular grade? Can you see how your students fared with the writing portion of the test? Are there tests such as DIBELS that help you understand the progress of your younger students?

As we first began to synthesize information about assessments in our own school, we used an assessment matrix to gather all this information. The matrix categories represent the areas of fluency, writing, comprehension, and word knowledge, as illustrated on the Chicago Reading Initiative's website (www.cri.cps.k12.il.us). Although we were not able fill this sheet out in the beginning of the year, we return to it consistently as we find it a good way to get teachers to think about how and what they are assessing both individually and as a school. We use the categories of word knowledge, comprehension, fluency, and writing to address the different areas of students' literacy. Of course, in many situations, one assessment may cover several of these categories. The assessment matrix becomes a tool that encourages conversations between various grade levels. Figure 13 is a sample data overview chart for second grade, and Figure 14 is a sample data overview chart for third grade (see Appendix A for a reproducible version of this chart, as well as a Schoolwide Data Inventory Planner).

The overview will allow you a quick look at the type of assessments that your school utilizes. In some situations, it will also make apparent what areas your school may not be assessing. Of course, once you fill in the information in the matrix, you may wonder, How are these assessments used? Are these assessments formative or summative

Figure 13. Sample Data Overview Chart for Second Grade

Grade 2	Quarter 1	Quarter 2	Quarter 3	Quarter 4
Word knowledge	DIBELS (ST) Developmental spelling list (SW) Sight word check (GL)	DIBELS (ST) Developmental spelling list (SW) Sight word check (GL)	Developmental spelling list (SW) Sight word check (GL)	DIBELS (ST) Developmental spelling list Sight word check (GL)
Comprehension assessments	Running records Oral questions answered verbally (literal/inferential; TM)	Running records Oral questions answered verbally (TM)	Running records Oral questions answered in written form (TM)	Running record Questions answered in written form (TM)
Fluency	DIBELS (ST)	DIBELS (ST)	Fluency checks (TM)	DIBELS (ST)
Writing	Prompt Narrative (TM) 6-Traits rubric	Prompt Expository (TM)	Prompt Free write (TM)	Prompt Expository (TM)

Note. GL = grade-level assessment; ST = state test; SW = schoolwide assessment; TM = teacher-made assessment.

Figure 14. Sample Data Overview Chart for Third Grade

Grade 3	Quarter 1	Quarter 2	Quarter 3	Quarter 4
Word knowledge	Developmental spelling list Sight word check Vocabulary in context (TM)	Developmental spelling list Sight word check Vocabulary in context (TM)	Developmental spelling list Sight word Vocabulary in context (TM)	Developmental spelling list Sight word Vocabulary in context (TM)
Comprehension	Running record State benchmark test Questions Extended response to reading passage	Running record State benchmark test Questions Extended response to reading passage	Running record Questions Extended response to reading passage (TM) ISAT exam	Running record Questions Extended response to reading passage (TM)
Fluency	Fluency checks	Fluency checks	Fluency checks	Fluency checks
Writing	Narrative Prompt (TM)	Expository Prompt (TM)	ISAT Expository	Letter writing Prompt (TM)

Note. GL = grade-level assessment; ST = state test; SW = schoolwide assessment; TM = teacher-made assessment.

measures noted on the report card? What type of regularized methods do they have for assessing progress between quarters? This organizer sheet is meant for the type of data that teachers measure consistently and use as indicators of student learning.

As you look through the data inventory chart, two categories of questions will most likely occur. The first category is questions that address assessment from a whole-school perspective. These questions might include the following:

- What type of assessments do teachers use at the various grade levels? What do they assess? How is this information used as a school?
- Do teachers find these assessments useful for their teaching?
- How do teachers share data? How often do they do so?
- How often do teachers analyze data?

- Do teachers use common assessments? If so, when and for what skills?
- Are teachers familiar with the assessments of grades above or below them?
- Does formative data follow students as they progress through various grades?
- Do teachers share a common language when describing formative data?

From the whole-school data, you will begin to narrow in on grade levels and ultimately classroom data.

The trends you notice will probably inspire ideas for professional development workshops, agenda for grade-level meetings, and foci for study groups. The assessment matrix can also serve as a springboard for conversations with your principal about schoolwide data conversations or the goals for professional development.

At the same time as you begin to see areas that will need further investigation on the school level, you can notice information about individual teachers and grade levels. This insight into grade-level data, in turn, directs your coaching as you begin to ask further questions, such as the following:

- What type of data do teachers use at this grade level? How are the assessments aligned to state standards?
- Do teachers use this formative data in their planning?
- Do teachers assess comprehension, word knowledge, fluency, and writing? How do they use this information for planning?
- How do teacher-made assessments take into account state standards? Do assessments measure what teachers want?
- How and with whom do teachers share information about these assessments?
- Do parents understand goals of assessments?

Finally, as we gather this information grade by grade, we make our own notation next to areas that we believe are used summatively and could better be used as formative information to guide the course of instruction. This assessment sheet can be the starting point in terms of schoolwide, individual, or grade-level coaching.

Data Mining Scenarios

Data are most valuable in that they help lead you to make informed decisions. Here, we present three situations where data were the springboard for schoolwide instructional decisions at our school. In each of these cases, after reviewing the data that were available, an authentic need, based on analysis of data, steered our coaching. In each of these scenarios, formative information guided the work we did as a whole school and our individual coaching sessions with teachers.

Scenario 1: We have no common assessments. As we began to look through our assessment matrix, we realized that teachers lacked a common assessment in early grades. Some teachers used running records, others had created their own assessments, and others used assessments from basal readers. Each teacher defined reading on grade level as something different from the others. Some might report the data in terms of a letter based on Fountas and Pinnell's (2001) guided reading system, while others might report as a percentage correct on a test. The lack of common language was symptomatic of an ambiguity about what it meant to be on grade level. Without any shared way of describing student performance or agreed-upon grade-level targets, when teachers talked about students, they had difficulty sharing information with one another and helping parents understand the message.

How we used it for formative coaching. The decision to institute running records as a shared assessment for students in grades K–5 was just one way we began to establish a common language of describing student reading. It helped us to identify clear targets for reading and comprehension for each grade level. After a few professional development sessions, we began our job-embedded coaching by seeking out teachers to work with individually in their classrooms in order to demonstrate how to conduct and analyze these assessments and plan for instruction.

As the data from the running records began to be reported, it became clear that there were many grade levels that had students that were reading way below and way above grade level. This led us to look more closely into the teaching methods and begin to focus our coaching on how teachers could support and challenge, through reading groups and other differentiated instruction techniques, learners who read on vastly different reading levels. In an effort to learn more about this topic, our principal let us create schoolwide learning walks that allowed groups of teachers to be a part of focused classroom visits that investigated the practices of differentiation throughout the school. For further information about schoolwide changes and the development of a professional learning community based on formative data, see Chapter 5.

Scenario 2: Formative classroom data are lost as students progress year after year. Each year, teachers at our school accumulated much knowledge about the students who sat in front of them. They could tell you their reading levels, how fluent they were as readers, and what progress they had made with writing. Yet, at the end of the year, much of this data was tossed or taken home. We knew that we were losing valuable instructional time as teachers spent time carefully trying to figure out the levels of their students. Interestingly, what students seemed to know the year before somehow disappeared the next year. Although the fifth-grade teacher may have sworn that she taught and saw evidence of a student using details to support his ideas in his essays, the next year that knowledge had simply vanished.

How we used it for formative coaching. We realized that we needed to hold on to what we knew about student work to help teachers plan their instruction for their next class and to hold students accountable for what they had previously learned. We started by asking teachers to keep work folders for students that shed light on them as readers and writers. We offered suggestions and then with our literacy team we standardized what should be kept year after year. We developed a system of transferring work folders at the end of the year to the students' new teachers.

As we began to look at the folders, we noticed that not all teachers interpreted work the same way. While some teachers might have felt a particular piece was on grade level, another teacher might disagree. We also saw that some teachers gave in-depth feedback to students about their work by marking up papers, others included rubrics, and still others simply put a check on the piece of work. We realized that we needed to spend time explicitly defining grade-level standards and discuss various techniques to provide students with meaningful feedback.

Scenario 3: Our students are struggling with higher order thinking.
Both teacher input and standardized test data confirmed that our students were struggling with inferential thought. You could see that going beyond the text was difficult for them both in formalized testing situations and during in-class conversations. Our students were reading words, but they were not thinking deeply about the text. All the teachers lamented about this challenge, but none more loudly than our third-grade teachers who knew their students would be held back based on their ability to answer these types of questions during the Illinois Standards Achievement Test (ISAT).

When we looked at the assessment matrix, we noticed that teachers used a variety of measures to assess comprehension. As we began to talk to them individually about these assessments, teachers reported many similar struggles. It seemed that students were often confused by what the questions about a text were really asking. Where was this information for the answer supposed to come from?

How we used it for formative coaching. Based on what teachers were saying, we spent a lot of time listening to our students make meaning from text. We would often ask them to tell us their thinking or explain why they answered a question in a particular way. Our youngest students were often confused about how much of their own thinking they could put in the answer when asked to draw a conclusion about how a character had changed in the story or what the author's purpose was in writing a specific text. The difficulty our school was having with inferential thinking led us as a school to adopt Question–Answer Relationships (QAR; Raphael, Highfield, & Au, 2006), which is a strategy to help students determine the relationship between the question and the answer. QAR also helped our students read actively by cultivating the use of reading strategies. This led us to spend much time in classrooms, working with teachers and students on how to use these strategies. To look at how data inform individual coaching, see Chapters 3 and 4.

REFLECTING AND EXTENDING

In this chapter, we discussed the beginning steps to coaching. For a coach to be successful, he or she must seek out opportunities to get to know teachers and form relationships with them. There are a number of techniques to build relationships, from a quick visit to a teacher's classroom to the development of an after-school professional development program to book groups about literacy topics. While learning about the teachers you work with, it is also important to learn about the data available in your school and how it is used.

We presented the Data Overview Chart as one way of synthesizing how teachers assess students. This, then, can be used to begin conversations about how student assessments are used to inform instruction.

In the next chapter, we investigate the process of using student work to begin one-on-one coaching.

QUESTIONS TO CONSIDER

1. What strengths do you bring to coaching? What areas do you think will be challenging?
2. How will you prepare to meet those challenges?
3. What are ways that you develop relationships with teachers in your school?
4. How familiar are you with the data available at your school? How is it used to inform instruction?
5. How has data informed your coaching?

CHAPTER 3

The Game Plan

Imagine This!

It is a busy Tuesday morning when you run into Ms. S in the hallway. Ms. S is a third-year teacher and always eager to talk about instruction. You have made a point to make a few quickstop meetings with her after school to talk. After several casual conversations, you feel that you are beginning to get to know her as a teacher. You greet Ms. S with a smile and ask how she is doing. She stops for a moment and then sighs. "I'm fine, I guess. But my students are just not getting essay writing. I've done everything I can think of, and the writing is still poor." The door has swung open. You ask if she would like to meet to talk about their work and brainstorm some teaching ideas. She agrees. Excited, you search through your files and pull out all of your resources on essay writing.

That afternoon you meet with Ms. S and she brings you a pile of 30 essays. "You see," she tells you, "they are not getting it." As you flip through the papers, you try not to look overwhelmed. You recognize organizational problems across the board. As you look closely, you notice some students have major grammatical errors in their assignments, while others seem stifled by the formulaic style of writing she has instructed her students to use in order to make sure they explain their ideas. She is right; the students are struggling but not for the same reasons. Should you volunteer to model a lesson on essay writing? You know that she is willing to work with you, but where do you start? How can you use this work in a meaningful fashion without it overwhelming her or you? You have worked hard to get to this point where teachers feel comfortable talking about curriculum and instruction. But now what?

A s you begin to form relationships with teachers, you will probably feel more comfortable talking to them informally, offering suggestions, even modeling lessons and dropping by to help work with students. While the support you offer may be valuable, is it enough to propel a school or even a classroom toward a higher standard of literacy learning? How can you develop a game plan that can help teachers in their classroom so that it will positively influence student learning?

The primary challenge in coaching teachers is improving student performance. The trick with coaching is building a bridge that connects you, the teacher, and students in a way that does not necessitate your daily presence in each classroom (see Figure 15). As a coach, you can demonstrate teaching strategies, lend resources, and work with individual students, but perhaps the most effective support you can provide teachers is the understanding of how formative work can help them teach more effectively. It is the habit of using student data that you hope to inspire in them. For many teachers, this type of assessment-based planning can necessitate a change in perspective

In your coaching, you will encounter teachers who base their planning and instruction on opening a textbook to the first page or relying on a tried-and-true teaching technique. Consider yourself as a teacher. How did you decide what to teach?

As you read this chapter, you will become acquainted with techniques and protocols that you can use to make meaning of formative data as you begin your coaching. The methods can be used in your individual mentoring of teachers or in collaborative groups.

Figure 15. Relationship Between Coach, Teacher, and Student

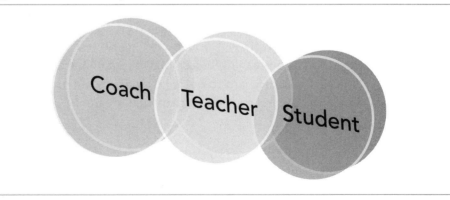

Getting Prepared for One-on-One Coaching

As you begin to get ready for your individual coaching session, let's return for a moment to the formative data analysis cycle (see Figure 4 on page 17 in Chapter 1). As a coach you may support teachers through some or all of these steps. It will not always be the case that you will begin your coaching with the goals of a lesson. Sometimes, a teacher might approach you with a stack of running records and ask you for help understanding what to do. Another time, you might meet with a teacher as they are planning what to teach next quarter. Other times, a teacher might ask you to assist with planning a lesson to help students see the connection between writing and their own lives. The cycle should remain flexible and accommodate the needs of the teachers, students, and coach.

Although starting your coaching with formative information in front of you may be desirable, it is important to not be rigid in your approach with teachers. Some teachers may not feel comfortable sharing their student work with you initially. Getting to that point might take further development of your relationship. Perhaps demonstrating a lesson in their classroom or working with a group of students might show them that you are willing to open yourself up as well (see Table 7 for ways to support teachers during the formative coaching cycle).

Before you begin meeting with teachers, we recommend preparing yourself by looking through grade-level standards and getting to know the resources in your school. Most states have their standards online, but as you have probably come to see, this doesn't mean that these standards are always clearly articulated to teachers or students. If you read through your standards and are still left feeling unclear, the next step may be to look at samples of state tests. Although we are not proponents of teaching to the tests, sometimes these assessments can make grade-level standards more clear by demonstrating the length of passages students at a specific grade level might have to read, what kind of vocabulary they will likely encounter, and what kind of inferences they should be able to draw from their readings. State tests are just another source of data to understand grade-level goals and standards.

If your school is using a textbook, looking at the differences in types of reading and associated learning tasks may also help you start to notice the expectations of each grade. Other helpful resources to help prepare you for formative coaching are as follows:

Table 7. How Coaches Can Support Teachers During Different Phases of the Formative Coaching Cycle

Phase of the cycle	Questions to consider during coaching	Example
Step 1: Determine goal for learning	What are grade-appropriate goals? How can goals be broken down? How can teachers translate standards into learning activities? How can teachers make goals clear to students? How can teachers make goals clear to other teachers?	Coach meets with sixth-grade teachers to review writing standards. After looking at state-level standards, they decide to articulate the goal to teachers and students by showing examples of sixth-grade on-level writing.
Step 2: Identify formative assessment	How can teachers assess student understanding? What kind of data can I collect? What types of assessments are available at my school? How can teachers develop their own? What criteria will teachers use to assess students? How does this relate to their goals?	Coach meets with fourth-grade teacher, and teacher identifies expository essay as a formative assessment that she will use to understand students' writing. Coach and teacher discuss criteria that will be used to assess work.
Step 3: Plan/teach lesson	How can the teacher plan effective lessons? What strategies will help students acquire the goal? How can the lesson be broken down or differentiated?	Coach and teacher discuss lesson. Coach brings in mentor texts, refers teacher to helpful websites, and develops plan to coteach lesson.
Step 4: Dig into the data	How can teachers collaborate around student work? How can teachers determine students' needs based on instruction?	Coach meets with grade-level team and demonstrates protocol for analyzing student work. Coach and teacher determine needs of students.
Step 5: Provide feedback	How can teachers let students know about their strengths and challenges? What teaching strategies might work to help the progress of students above, on target, and below grade level?	Coach brainstorms feedback strategies for groups of students. Coach makes a plan to collaborate with teacher around future lessons. Cycle begins again.

- *The Differentiated Classroom: Responding to the Needs of All Learners* by Carol Ann Tomlinson

- *The Continuum of Literacy Learning, Grades K–8* by Gay Su Pinnell and Irene C. Fountas

- *The Constructivist Leader* by Linda Lambert, Deborah Walker, Diane P. Zimmerman, Joanne E. Cooper, Morgan Dale Lambert, Mary E. Gardner, and Margaret Szabo

- *The Facilitator's Book of Questions* by David Allen and Tina Blythe

- *Collaborative Analysis of Student Work: Improving Teaching and Learning* by Georgea M. Langer, Amy B. Colton and Loretta S. Goff

Building Your Knowledge About Differentiation

Although looking at student work is invigorating, it can also be overwhelming. As you look through it, what becomes evident is that each running record, each developmental spelling list, each journal entry is saying something specific about that student's needs. And, not surprisingly, the students do not all need the same thing. The one-size-fits-all lesson plan does not fit when you look at the varying levels and needs illustrated through student work before you. Yet certainly that cannot mean that teachers would need to develop 25 different lesson plans to suit all of the learners in their room.

According to Tomlinson (1999), when teachers respond to the different needs among their learners, they are differentiating. Although most teachers recognize the need to differentiate at times, actually planning to do so can be overwhelming. It is hard enough to plan one good lesson for everyone—how can a teacher be asked to think about individual student needs with every lesson?

Differentiation is often discussed in terms of small-group or individual instruction, but differentiation can also be done in whole-class settings. Sometimes, the term *differentiation* can be off-putting because it sounds like something new that will require more time and energy. Connecting this type of planning to what they already do in the classroom makes the concept of differentiation easier to incorporate. **Many teachers may not be conscious that they are, in fact, differentiating their instruction**

throughout the day. The following are some simple ways teachers differentiate every day:

- Asking a student to move closer to board or enlarging a text
- Allowing extra time for a student who writes slowly
- Introducing a new vocabulary word through a kinesthetic approach
- Moving yourself closer to a student who may need more support or have trouble focusing
- Pairing students
- Allowing for student choice
- Providing multiple opportunities for students to express understanding
- Creating visuals to help explain oral directions
- Rewording or rephrasing
- Allowing students to choose how they would like to synthesize their learning
- Breaking down a particular skill or assignment into component parts
- Incorporating independent reading during the day

When you begin to look at data, whether it is scores on a test or a writing assignment, it becomes clear that learners are all very different in the way they think. Data must be looked at from multiple perspectives to get a good understanding of each learner and his or her challenges and strengths.

Take, for example, the following passage given to a group of second-grade students:

> The Goliath frog can be found along rivers in Africa. It spends most of its day in fast-moving water and near waterfalls. It likes to eats insects, fish, and other small animals.

As the teacher conferred with the learners about the passage, she asked them what they thought the word *insects* meant.

Learner A couldn't decode the words. She had no other strategies but to sound out words she didn't know. She did not look at the pictures or charts to help her gain meaning about the passage. When the passage was read aloud to her, she was able to figure out the meaning of the word *insects*.

Learner B was able to decode the words in the passage. He constructed meaning based on prior knowledge. He knew that frogs ate bugs, so he hypothesized that is what *insects* meant. He also noticed the phrase *other small animals* and realized that could be a clue to what *insect* meant.

Learner C could decode but lacked comprehension of the passage. She was able to say the words aloud but was not able to answer simple questions or summarize. Even when the teacher showed her how to figure out what *insects* means by using clues in the sentence, she guessed water when asked to explain the word *insects* again.

When you consider these three students, it is clear that they have very different learning needs. This is where differentiation comes into play. At its most basic level, differentiation is the process whereby a teacher responds to the variation among learners. As teachers plan lessons for individuals or groups of learners, they modify their instruction almost unconsciously. However, the art of differentiating instruction is based on careful planning and forethought.

Tomlinson (1999) categorizes differentiated instruction into four areas that can be modified to support learners: (1) content, (2) process, (3) product, and (4) learning environment—the way the surrounding classroom responds to the learner's needs (see Figure 16). These categories often provide a framework for thinking about how to modify the curriculum to meet the needs of students. Often when differentiation is discussed, it is thought about as techniques to help struggling learners. Yet differentiation is as important to your struggling readers as it is to your most sophisticated ones.

One fourth-grade teacher, Ms. M, offers the following explanation for how she differentiates instruction throughout the day:

> Sometimes differentiation means where I put them [the students] or where I am standing. Other times it might be the book they are reading, the way I ask them to respond to questions, or if I direct their focus to one specific paragraph instead of asking them to look through a whole text.

Figure 16. Four Areas of Differentiated Instruction

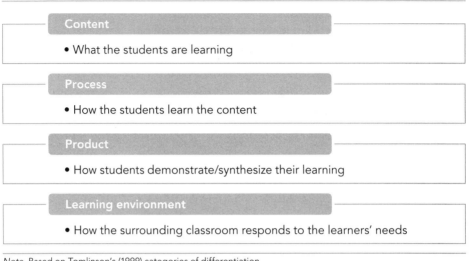

Content
- What the students are learning

Process
- How the students learn the content

Product
- How students demonstrate/synthesize their learning

Learning environment
- How the surrounding classroom responds to the learners' needs

Note. Based on Tomlinson's (1999) categories of differentiation.

This teacher learns about her students not only from reading assessments but also by asking them to write about themselves as learners, saying, "I want to know what they feel they are good at, their fears, and their goals."

Differentiating Your Coaching

Mostly, when we think about differentiation, it is in terms of meeting students' needs. However, as you begin to meet with teachers, it will become clear that you will need to vary your approach to respond to the needs, experiences, emotions, contexts, and interests of the teachers you are mentoring—differentiating your coaching for teachers. Often, we are not aware of all these factors. Sometimes, you might be met with a cool response from a teacher when you offer to work on lessons with her. Before jumping to conclusions, consider how she may have considered your offer. Does she think that this means she isn't doing a good job? Does she have more pressing matters that she needs to attend to? Is she concerned this will monopolize her planning time? When beginning your work with a teacher, there are many factors that can affect how your coaching on any individual day will go. As you plan your sessions, consider the following factors that can affect your meetings:

1. Environment: Where does the meeting take place? How are you positioned during your discussion? Who is else is present?
2. Context: What happened earlier that day? How much time do you have to meet? What else is the teacher trying to accomplish during this time?
3. Perspective: What type of experience does the teacher have with being coached? How do they view the process? Are they comfortable sharing information with someone outside the classroom? Are they comfortable reflecting one on one, or in larger groups?
4. Knowledge: What type of knowledge do they have about this area? What are their strengths as a teacher? What are their challenges?

Meetings can be affected by any number of factors, and although you cannot always know all of these situations, it often plays a very real role in the way your coaching sessions play out. Just imagine the difference in a coaching conversation about students' essays in the case of a teacher who feels that a coach's main purpose is to critique the teacher.

It takes time to get to know people and their teaching style. It also takes time to analyze student work. Coaching takes patience, and there will most likely be times when you will receive a mandate from your district or principal to have teachers follow a certain instructional method immediately. Imagine the scenario where your district decides that all teachers should have students keep writing portfolios. The district will provide professional development for the teachers, but you will be in charge of coaching them in their classrooms about how to use portfolios. As you develop a plan, your approach will naturally differ for individual teachers based on their experience and the students in their classroom. For one teacher the professional development they receive and feedback from you might be enough to experiment with writing workshop, while other teachers will require day-to-day classroom help, and still others might resist changing their writing curriculum at all.

When you meet to discuss student work with teachers, it is important to think carefully about the understanding and experience the teacher will bring to the meeting. Considering some of the following questions can help you plan how best to structure your meeting.

1. Is the teacher familiar with the difference between evaluating student work for a grade versus analyzing it as a formative assessment of what the student understands? Teachers are under pressure to assign students a grade. Mostly, when they look at student work it is to evaluate it and decide on a letter or number grade. However, this is definitely *not* the purpose of looking at work with a teacher when you are conducting formative coaching. The purpose is to analyze the students' strengths and weaknesses to determine the next course of action. The need to assign a grade can be distracting and can lead to a superficial analysis of the student work. Therefore, making the distinction between analyzing student work and evaluating it for a grade is important.

When you first begin to meet with teachers, you will want to make sure that you are very clear about the purpose of looking at student work together. Help them to understand that data will serve as a tool for analyzing what students can do and for developing future instruction. It is often the case with pressure to assign a grade that teachers can feel limited in the amount of time they have to give to such analysis. Therefore, it is usually wiser to start by only looking at one or two pieces of student work rather than work from the whole class. Once you have demonstrated how analyzing formative assessments will be helpful, it is often the teacher who will want to look through the work.

2. What is the goal of meeting with this teacher? How can discussing student work be a part of this goal? Before you meet with the teacher, it is good to discuss his or her goal. Does the teacher want to look at the work of the whole class, of an individual, or of a group of students? Knowing this will help you organize your time.

As you begin to plan for your meeting, think about how looking at student work can help the teacher meet his or her goal. Sometimes, there is a mismatch between the type of student work the teacher has chosen and the teacher's previously specified goal. For example, if a teacher wants to discuss comprehension and then selects to look only at one-minute timed fluency reads, this might not be a good formative assessment of the students' ability to comprehend a text. Yet even when formative data and the goals of the analysis do not align, you can use this situation to help teachers reflect on their teaching with the formative coaching cycle. Sometimes, in fact, teachers need to look through the work briefly as part of a preliminary process of even choosing or narrowing a goal for the coaching meeting. In this case, having general questions can help lead the teachers to make observations about the student work. The following are some question stems you can use for this purpose:

- What did you notice about…?
- What are some of your thoughts about…?
- What/how might…?
- What are some possible…?

Garmston (2000) argues that some of the most important skills for a staff developer are questions that encourage teachers to think from multiple perspectives. Meditative questions, as he refers to them, are open-ended and judgment free and use language that is exploratory. These questions can help teachers identify areas on which they would like to focus their efforts. Having question stems available when you first meet with a teacher can help you begin your conversations.

3. How does the teacher feel about sharing student work with others? Some teachers may feel uncomfortable about sharing their students' work with you. They may feel like the work their students are doing is being used as an evaluation. For example, one teacher always told us about the wonderful writing students were doing in her class. But then when we asked her to share the actual pieces with us and other teachers, the work was never available. Instead, she held the pile of papers close to her and handed us lesson plans to discuss. For this teacher, sharing student work was something she was not comfortable doing.

There are a few ways to address this dilemma. Sometimes, simply asking a teacher to share something that he or she is proud that the students were able to do is a way to open the door to begin to talk about students' work. Starting with students' strengths rather than discussing what they cannot do is a good start in getting to know individual learners. For teachers who shy away from even revealing their students' strengths, you might look at samples of student work that are not from their classroom and begin the process of analyzing this formative data collaboratively.

4. Does the teacher have a tool (rubric, checklist, criteria) for analyzing the work? When you begin to look through student work, you will notice work that seems exemplary, average, and far below standard for students on that grade level. How are you making these assessments of the student work? Are there criteria that you are using to determine what students should know? Often, teachers have an image of what on-target grade-level work looks like.

For example, one teacher could quickly point out some student writing that was far below grade level. As we began to talk, though, it became apparent that she was unclear about what grade-level writing actually looked like. In her mind, she had a vague impression of it formed by years of teaching and reference to standards but not specific criteria. As she started to analyze the work, it became clear that without a clear vision in her mind, she could not provide models for her students. However, it is often difficult to articulate this to other teachers and, most importantly, students. When you begin to look at student output, how will you know at what level they should be achieving? Many schools stress the notion of academic rigor. But how does "rigor" look in the work of a third-grade class relative to a fourth-grade class or an eighth-grade class? You and the teacher should be able to articulate what you want to see. For teachers who are unfamiliar with analyzing work, you may want to bring samples of rubrics or checklists.

5. How will the teacher respond to finding out what the students need? The way you approach looking at student work will be shaped by the teacher's response to the process. For some, the process of analyzing student work as a formative assessment can be eye-opening; for others, it initially feels overwhelming. With some teachers, we noticed that this process encouraged them to rethink and reflect on their lessons and goals. They were happy to sit and spend time looking through a running record or analyzing the work in a Venn diagram. Looking at student work allowed teachers to better understand the students and their needs as learners. As exciting as some may find the process, others were less patient. First, doing this takes extra time, which is a precious commodity. It requires skill to analyze what they see in front of them and then plan future instruction. Finally, it serves as the ultimate reality check as teachers begin to see that simply because they taught a lesson on a specific skill, this does not mean that students can apply it. On one hand, it is enlightening to begin to understand what type of instruction the students need, and on the other, it can be intimidating to realize that following a teachers' guide day by day may not be the best way of instructing learners.

As you coach teachers around student work, it is important to be aware of the varied responses individuals will have. One cannot always assume that it will be the inexperienced teachers who will be the most intimidated or unskilled in analyzing student work. Nor is it correct to jump to the conclusion that a seasoned teacher will be unwilling to make changes to their instruction. It will take time to learn about how people respond to meeting with you (see Table 8 for suggestions on preparing for your meetings with teachers).

Introducing the Cycle Into Your Coaching

Often when you begin to work with teachers, they may express interest in your helping to support them on teaching a specific skill or strategy to students. Usually, conversations about instruction begin in very general terms. A teacher might say, "I need help with incorporating vocabulary instruction into reading," "My students are reading, but I don't think they

Table 8. Guidelines for Preparing for Meetings With Teachers

Preparation questions	Prepare
What is the goal of meeting with this teacher? What has she expressed interest in discussing? How will looking at student work help the teacher to meet her goal?	It may be that looking at the particular type of student work may not meet the specific goal of the meeting. In this case, you may want to state this to the teacher and discuss a course of action to pursue.
Does the teacher know how to analyze this type of student work? Does she have a tool for evaluating it? Will you need to provide one?	If the teacher is unfamiliar with analyzing student work, you may want to model how you look at it. You may also want to bring examples of how to evaluate work (rubrics, checklists).
How will she respond to finding out what the students need?	For some teachers, looking at what students need may be overwhelming. How can you present it in a more manageable fashion?
What does the teacher understand and feel about differentiating her curriculum?	As you plan your next steps, evaluate how the teacher has responded. What are your next steps to support instruction?

are paying attention to their books. Can you tell me what the problem is?" or "J reads on a first-grade level but is in fourth grade. What should I be doing with him?" As you begin to talk to the teacher, you should ask questions to narrow down the support needed. Sometimes, you may both determine that the teacher needs your assistance with analyzing student work, but as you begin to look at the formative assessments, you realize that the assessments may not actually allow students to demonstrate their knowledge.

Acquainting teachers with the formative data analysis cycle (see Figure 4 on page 17 in Chapter 1) is a way of talking about how you can help them. Although teachers may not be thinking about instruction in this way, it helps to center your discussions on student improvement. We use this visual as a way to introduce the cycle and discuss where the teacher is in his or her instruction and what types of support we might offer.

However, there are also times when we want to keep coaching more informal and we do not show teachers this graphic. In situations when you first work with a teacher who may be still unsure of your role, the cycle may look like more of a commitment to working with you than they are ready to make at that point. In these cases, we recommend using the cycle yourself to determine how best to support the teacher and sharing it when you feel your relationship and role is more established. This is a simple way that you can differentiate your coaching that takes into account the individuals with whom you work. No matter whether you choose to show the teacher the cycle or not, it is a good idea to keep the steps in the back of your mind. And one aspect always remains a constant in our coaching: the idea that coaching conversations should be grounded in formative data. Guidelines for introducing the formative coaching cycle are as follows:

1. Show a visual if appropriate.
2. Explain purpose of cycle.
3. Connect what the teacher already does in terms of planning with the different phases of the cycle.
4. Explain how you can support the teacher throughout the cycle.
5. Determine goals of lesson and goal of coaching.
6. Allow the teacher to ask questions and give feedback about the cycle.

In the following example, the coach introduces the coaching cycle to a teacher with whom she has casually worked before:

Coach: So, I wanted to show you this new planning tool I am using to help me figure out ways to support you in the classroom. As a classroom teacher, these are all the things you do on a daily basis: figure out the goal of your lesson, teach it, and then determine if you think students have understood it. [Coach points to the cycle as she explains.] My role is to figure out how I can best support you during the different parts of your teaching. So, for example, you were telling me that you are concerned because students seem not to be paying attention to their reading. What is the goal that you are trying to accomplish?

Teacher: I want them to be actively reading. I've done a lot of lessons on all sorts of explicit reading strategies, but I don't think they are doing this. When they get to the end of the story, they can't tell me much about what they have read, not even the most basic parts.

Coach: How do you assess comprehension?

Teacher: I hold conferences with them during their reading. Also, I ask them to answer questions that require using details from the story.

Coach: Okay. So that's your formative assessment. Do you have samples of the answers that they wrote or any notes that you jotted down while you confer with them?

Teacher: Yes, just some informal notes and the answers that students wrote to the questions.

Coach: Okay, how about we start there? Let's look at both of these together and see if we can understand what the students are doing. From there, we can figure out if we need to find out more information and what lessons might help with their comprehension.

Although the teacher is ready to start brainstorming ideas for lessons, the coach starts by asking the teacher to look at work collaboratively. It is by doing this that they can begin to make clear the learning goals and, most importantly, what meaning students are constructing.

How does formative information help you in your coaching? How will this data assist you in the formative analysis cycle in identifying a target for instruction, developing a lesson, or assessing student understanding? We believe that formative information can be part of every step of the cycle. As you look at Table 9, you can see how formative information is an inherent part of the different phases of the cycle, from identifying a goal to deciding what the next steps will be.

Many times, literacy coaches do not start working with teachers at the very first step of the cycle. It is not uncommon for a teacher to invite you during stage 3 to help plan or teach a lesson. Regardless of the point you begin your coaching, it is important to ground the discussion in formative information and explain the process of how you can both determine what works for students in their classroom. Although it is not always the case that when you meet with a teacher they will have formative information to work with, we suggest sending them a note prior to your meeting so that they might collect some student data.

Table 9. Promoting Formative Analysis Throughout the Stages of the Formative Coaching Cycle

Phase of cycle	Questions to promote formative analysis throughout cycle
Step 1: Determine goal for teaching	Look at formative data. What does the student work show that students need? How does this influence the goals of the lesson?
Step 2: Identify formative assessment	Look at previous work from students. What assessments have been helpful in determining student understanding of the skill? Thinking about the formative information you have available, are the same assessments good indicators of understanding/application for all students?
Step 3: Plan/teach lesson	What does previous student work show about the way individual students learn in the class? How can you fit your instruction to match the learning style of students?
Step 4: Dig into data	What does the student work indicate about student understanding? Was this type of instruction effective? If so, for whom? Was the assessment a good indicator of student understanding?
Step 5: Provide feedback	What will you do with this information? Will you move on to a new goal, break the class into groups, or continue to review this skill with the entire class? How will you let students know about their progress?

Strategies for Understanding Formative Work

Once you have started to dig into the student work with teachers, there are many ways to make sense of formative data. Some of the techniques will be determined by the actual data sources you use and, of course, your purposes. For example, you might want to examine one particular feature in a group of essays to assess student understanding. You might look at work over time and investigate how a particular group did with similar assignments. Perhaps a teacher is concerned about an individual student in the class. In this case, you might look at multiple assessments to get an idea of the student as a learner. Always, the technique you use is determined by the goal of your meeting.

Sometimes there are situations when you need to look at the work before you can even determine your purpose. Perhaps just shuffling through papers, scanning fluency reads, or glancing at misspelled words on a developmental spelling list can begin to give you a purpose. Making sense of student work takes patience and creativity as you carefully analyze what you see. It means acknowledging that your understanding of the work is shaped by your perspective, goals, and expectations. Approaching the analysis of student work without a strategy can lead to frustration and confusion. Although it sometimes takes a first glance at the work to decide what exactly you are looking at, it is best to have a plan in mind from the start. In your initial attempts at looking at student work, you might try and analyze every single student's piece. With 25 journal entries in front of you and an unclear focus, the process seems daunting, and most likely there wouldn't be enough time to make any sense of it.

Though the techniques you use to look at the work depend upon the students, the adult learner, the goal, and the context of your meeting, the following four general strategies can be employed to help organize and make sense of what you see during your meetings with teachers:

1. Quick sort: Sorting student work based on criteria into groups
2. Class impressions: Analyzing multiple sources of data from a group of learners to assess student understanding of a particular skill
3. Goal setting (or Individual Student Analysis Method [ISAM] Protocol): Looking at student work over time and developing goals from this data

4. Assignment analysis (or BEST Assignment Analysis): Analyzing the underlying skills that the assignment or assessment requires that students know

Underlying all of these techniques is a process we call "trendspotting." Trendspotting is simply a method of identifying similarities within an individual or group's formative data (see Figure 17). These similarities serve as guideposts to determine next steps. For example, if you notice that all individuals in a group of students struggled with understanding how to answer a particular question, this trend can alert you to the importance of analyzing the problem (as suggested in the assignment analysis strategy) and figuring out what might have been a stumbling block for them.

We describe each of the strategies—quick sort, class impressions, goal setting, and assignment analysis (see Table 10)—in the sections that follow, and in Appendix B we provide a detailed protocol, or set of prescribed steps, that assign the coach and teacher specific roles to help both make meaning of student data using each strategy. A protocol is a structure

Figure 17. Trendspotting

Table 10. Using Formative Data Strategies

Technique	Purpose	Type of analysis	Questions to ask
Quick sort	Good for initial discussions of student work Begins discussion on what you expect student to know/demonstrate	Work done by small group Work done by whole class	How did you make these piles? What criteria did you use to place the student work? Were there any pieces that were hard to put into a group? Why?
Class impressions	A macroscopic view (usually around test data reported in percentages) where teachers can determine strengths and weaknesses as a class in certain areas	Groups	Based on the numbers, what areas do you think you need to focus on as a whole class? What do students need to do to be successful at X? What test-taking skills do students need?
Goal setting	Used to develop goals for individual students and to analyze strengths and weaknesses	Individuals	What are strengths and challenges for this student? What are goals that you have set for this learner? How do you measure this student's progress?
Assignment analysis	Used to begin discussion about what the assignment (formative assessment) is asking student to do and to help uncover subskills within larger assignment	Individuals or groups	What are the skills that make up this assignment? What did you do while you were thinking about an answer for X? What steps do you think students need to do in order to be successful with this assignment? What scaffolding will you supply them with?

that enables educators to look carefully and collaboratively at student and teacher work to learn from it (Allen, 2006). We find it helpful to distinguish between strategies and protocols. For example, if you work with a teacher to sort her students' work into a number of different piles, you are now using the quick sort as a strategy for analyzing work. However, if you and the teacher follow the prescribed steps that are described for using this strategy in Appendix B, the quick sort strategy becomes a protocol. The choices you make about which method to use will depend on your school environment and your goals after looking at data.

Although protocols may feel artificial at first, their purpose is to establish guidelines and build capacity to make meaning from data. For many teachers, this may be the first time they will be exposing their students' work to others. Opening the doors of the classroom ultimately can be a powerful tool for student learning, but it can also be frightening. As coaches, the protocols provide us with a structure and guide to help facilitate the difficult conversations that come up when analyzing and looking at student work collectively.

Quick Sort

When you first meet with a teacher who has not had much experience in analyzing student work as a formative assessment, he or she may not know exactly what to look at or how to use this information. One way of starting your conversation is through a technique called the quick sort (see Figure 18). Have teachers sort the student work into three piles: above standard, on standard, below standard. From this quick activity, you can then begin to investigate what informed the teacher's choices. What criteria was he or she using?

Take, for example, Ms. J, a first-grade teacher who has had her students write a response to a question about the book they read as a class. When you meet with Ms. J, you decide to use the Quick Sort Protocol (see Appendix B). You decide to use the steps of the protocol to help guide your analysis and maintain your focus. As Ms. J looks through the work, you begin by discussing the purpose of this formative data. You move to the next step where you begin to discuss criteria of judging it. Ms. J shows you her rubric and then begins to sort the work into the three piles. She starts her analysis with the work from her top group. She delves deeply into it, noting commonalities. The protocol keeps both you and Ms. J from

Figure 18. Quick Sort

making evaluations that are not based on actual evidence; it stops both of you from getting sidetracked into other conversations that lead away from your goals. Using the steps has helped guide your coaching conversation by keeping both of you focused on the data in front of you in order to plan your next steps.

Class Impressions

Sometimes it is good to get a holistic view of how the class is doing before delving into individual pieces of work. As teachers look through multiple formative assessments, they can use the template that accompanies the Class Impressions Protocol in Appendix B to mark down if they feel the product is below, on, or above grade level. After looking at a number of different measures of a particular skill or strategy, they can get an impression of how individuals or the class is doing in this area.

In the example in Table 11, the teacher wanted to see how her class was doing in the areas of word study and comprehension. After the results

Table 11. Class Impressions

Formative data	Word study				Comprehension			
	Content area words	Affix test	Word usage in writing	Fluency read	Verbal questioning of independent reading	Guided reading levels	Written questions for reading	Graphic organizer for story
Description of work	Sentences created with words from science (%)	Multiple-choice words (%)	6-traits rubric word fluency (1–6)	DIBELS one-minute probe (Fluency rate goal = 90 wpm)	Used rubric for retell of story (1–4)	Fountas & Pinnell reading levels (A–Z)	Assessed using state rubric (1–4)	Assessed for use of details to support answer (On or below standard)
Jack	100	95	5	106	3	T	3	On
Andrew	100	83	4	118	3	K	1	On
Monique	20	33	1	45	1	I	1	Below
Devon	60	83	2	10	1	U	3	Below
Clarisse	70	100	3	120	3	I	1	Below
Diamond	70	85	5	110	2	T	1	On
Priva	80	100	4	119	2	Q	2	On
Kris	80	50	2	74	1	U	2	On
Tammy	80	92	3	100	3	R	3	Below

of a state assessment on comprehension, the teacher was left wondering why her students did not fare better. She decided to use this state test as formative information and began asking many questions. She wanted to look at the variety of assessments she collected to see if there were patterns and also to determine if there was formative information that might help her understand her students' difficulty with comprehension.

For each student, she entered their scores for assessments she had done for both categories. This data ranged from more formal measures such as in-class multiple-choice exams to information she collected about the students' understanding of their independent reading books when she asked them questions aloud. Collecting it allowed her to form an impression of the students' comprehension from multiple sources.

The data were then color-coded to highlight patterns as well as anomalies. Looking at the data in this fashion often helps teachers ask questions and form hypotheses about their students' learning. For example, from this grid the teacher might wonder

- Do I see a connection between students' word knowledge and ability to comprehend texts?
- What kind of assessments did students struggle with? What did they do well on? Why do I think this?
- Are there students who perform erratically? Why is this?
- Are my assessments accurate measures of the skill? How can I tell?

These are just some of the questions that teachers begin to ask when they look at the data. From the most macroscopic perspective, you can begin to see groups of students emerge that need extra support or to be pushed further along.

Goal Setting—Individual Student Analysis Method (ISAM)

Looking at a student's work and analyzing it can help in setting goals, though this type of analysis can be time intensive. It may involve focusing on a specific feature or looking at the work as a whole to gain insight about the student. This method can be particularly helpful with students who are struggling. For this technique, we have developed the ISAM protocol to help guide your discussions with teachers (see Appendix B).

For example, after looking at a number of formative assessments, Ms. X determines that Marc is struggling. Although Marc is not far behind according to his running records, Ms. X notices that his fluency rate is very slow and that both his oral and written comprehension are also below grade level as determined by the rubric. She decides to look more closely and develop goals based on what she sees. She searches for trends in the work. As she looks at a running record, she notices that Marc repeatedly misses sight words. Looking at his fluency readings, she notices that this is also a problem. She questions whether the student's comprehension difficulties stem from not being able to get through the text. Based on this, she decides that she will have him focus on sight words so that by the end of the quarter he will be able to read the list fluently. She also decides to have him read simpler texts and then answer questions, as a further formative assessment.

Assignment Analysis—BEST Assignment Analysis

Another way to use student work is to look at what it says about the assignment. The work produced by students can provide insight into the underlying characteristics of an assignment and how to differentiate it for individual students (see the BEST Assignment Analysis Protocol in Appendix B). In some cases, when all students struggle with answering a question, it can be that the question itself is faulty or that students did not possess the prior knowledge to understand it. For example, in one comprehension test, students were asked how the character became wiser. The entire class struggled to answer this question. Under closer investigation, it became clear that the students did not know what *wise* meant. A few were able to piece it together from the context of the story, but many got confused by not knowing the term and could not continue with the question. The teacher decided to do another assessment where she changed the word from *wise* to *intelligent*. This rewording helped many of the students answer the question. This assessment made clear to the teacher that she had to work on vocabulary and on how to use context cues to figure out the meaning of a word.

Formative Data Techniques in Action: Coaching Case Studies

Let's take a more detailed look at how a coach might use formative data techniques and their corresponding protocols to support a teacher in the classroom. The section that follows offers two short profiles of coaching scenarios where the coach uses formative data techniques to understand the various needs of learners.

Teacher Profile #1: Ms. M

Number of years teaching: 5

Grade level: Third grade

Experience looking at student work as a formative assessment: Worked on literacy team last year

Relationship between coach and teacher: Friendly, although there has been no formal coaching interaction

Expected reaction to looking at student work: Positive

Focus: Looking at extended-response questions of third-grade students

The Scenario. Ms. M approaches you in the library one day and tells you that she feels her students are not able to write an extended, written response to reading comprehension questions, especially when the questions call for inferential thinking. Casually, she mentions some of the lessons she has done with her class and says she just can't understand why the students are not getting it. You ask if she would like to meet to look at her students' work and she agrees.

Preparing. Although Ms. M has been teaching for five years, you have never coached her before. You have seen her mentoring other teachers informally. She seems willing and capable of looking deeply into student work, though you are not sure if this is something she does regularly. Before you meet with her, you ask her to fill out a quick form, Looking at Student Work Check-In (see the sample in Figure 19 as well as the reproducible version in Appendix A), so that you can save time during your actual meeting. Although there is more information that you would like to know before meeting with her, you are also conscious of not taking

Figure 19. Sample Looking at Student Work Check-In

What type of work will we look at? When did students do this work? Students' answers to extend response questions. Students completed this assignment last week.

Under what circumstances did students do this work?
   ☑ Independently
   ☑ In groups/pairs   Students discussed work in
   ❑ With teacher support   pairs, but wrote independently
   ❑ Varied depending on learner

What is your goal in looking at this work? What do you particularly want to discuss? I want to help students answer inferential questions in written form and include evidence that supports their conclusions. I would like help with how I can develop lessons that will encourage students to support ideas with evidence from the text.
Do you have rubrics, criteria, or checklists that you use to assess this work? Yes, I am using the extended response rubric from the State. Students are familiar with this rubric.

too much of her time. Therefore, you ask if she can send you the work before the meeting so you can get some familiarity with the student responses. While looking at the samples independently, you see a variety of strengths and weaknesses. The students who struggle the most seem to lack basic comprehension of the text and do not answer the questions. Yet you can see that all of them have an opening and closing sentence and attempt to provide evidence. However, the textual evidence that they cite does not always support their ideas. You wonder if she has noticed the same thing.

Meeting. You begin your session by talking about the goals of coaching and showing Ms. M a graphic of the formative data analysis cycle (see Figure 4 on page 17 in Chapter 1). Although you feel comfortable being flexible—depending on her needs as you talk about the student work—you need to be aware of time and have set up the following plan:

1. Discuss goal of meeting

2. Quick sort

3. Discuss next steps for instruction

Ms. M takes out the student work and shows you a rubric she uses to grade the work. The rubric has been provided by the state and is based on students' ability to comprehend the text and support their answer with textual evidence. The question asks the students to describe how the character changed from the beginning to the end of the story. It requires students to make an inference and back up their ideas with support from the text. She shows you a sample paper and how she used the rubric to evaluate the work. You explain to her your plan and start by doing a quick sort exercise, looking for students that have performed above, on, or below grade level.

As you look through the work, you realize that there are no students who are performing above grade level, so you decide to redefine the categories. Your top group is now students who are performing close to or on grade level, the second group is below grade level, and the third group is far below grade level. Because you are aware that you have limited time, you do not look at the whole class. Instead you select 10 random examples. Because you have both looked at them before, you can move quickly through the exercise. Although the "the middle group" (below grade level) is the largest, you suggest starting with the students in the highest group (those that are on grade level) so that you can find pieces of writing that will serve as models. Again, your plan is a suggested protocol, which is open to change. Each time you suggest a method, you should explain your reasoning and ask for her input. In this beginning phase, you have decided to be more directive, primarily to save time (see Table 12 for a list of time-saving techniques).

Next you describe to her the process of trendspotting. The goal, you explain, is to get an overall impression and not (at this point) a fine level of detail. You decide to split the papers of the students in the middle group in half and notice positive and negative trends of the students who are achieving on grade level standards. In 10 minutes, you have looked through the papers and have begun discussing the work. Ms. M has written down "literal comprehension of the story" for strengths of this group. Most of the students can relay simple information from it. You ask her for an example, and she points to one paper and shows you how the student has referred to an event in the text. You agree and show another example from a different text.

Ms. M then goes on to say that the students struggle with making inferences. You ask for her an example and she pulls a paper. You begin to discuss why she thinks the top students in her class struggle with this skill. Maybe, she explains, they think that they are not allowed to say things that are not in the text. On one hand, she explains, we are saying to use textual evidence to support their ideas, and on the other, we are asking them to go beyond the text and make inferences. Maybe they are confused by these two messages. Both of you decide that the whole class could benefit by an explicit example of how one can infer things about characters or events in a story and support these conclusions with textual evidence.

Table 12. Time-Saving Techniques

- Look at the work and the rubric, if one is available, ahead of time
- Have teacher fill out the goal sheet before you meet
- Look at a sample of work rather than every student's work
- Split the papers so you look at half and the teacher looks at the other half

In the last few minutes, you discuss how she can provide feedback to her students. You talk about a number of techniques that she might use, and she decides that she will meet with the students in groups and provide feedback to them about the trends she saw (see Table 13). During this time, she will look at one paper with the group and do a think-aloud for the students while she analyzes what the student has done. Afterward, she will also have them share their own thinking about the original question and rewrite their response.

Follow-Up. In the last few minutes, you decide how to proceed with your findings. Ms. M tells you that she will do a few lessons in the next few days where she models how to make inferences. She asks for your help in

Table 13. Addressing Spotted Trends

Student group	What students can do	What students need further instruction in doing
Students near or at grade level	• Show understanding of the question and story • Able to provide details from story • Summarize parts of text necessary for answer • Make connections (not always relevant to answering question)	• Making inferences about the text • Understanding how to go beyond the text • Knowing the language necessary to make inferences about characters
Students below grade level	• Understand the question • Attempt answer • Summarize entire story (many student examples of this)	• Staying focused on answering the question (students sometimes got caught up in digressions) • Knowing the language necessary to make inferences about characters
Students far below grade level	• Attempt to answer question • Show sustained attention • Able to pick out some names and details from the story	• Comprehending text or question • Writing sentences about the story • Answering comprehension questions through a text read aloud to them or a story that is on their reading level

locating texts that might be appropriate to practice this skill. She also asks if you will look with her at the next group of student responses to discuss growth as well as listen to the students in her class.

The students arrive. Before you forget, you write a follow-up note where you summarize the meeting and place it in her mailbox (see Figure 20). You put a copy of the letter in your own file to document your work with Ms. M.

Teacher Profile #2: Mr. Z

Number of years teaching: 15+

Grade level: Fourth grade

Experience looking at student work as a formative assessment: Developed

Relationship between coach and teacher: Mr. Z is an experienced teacher who collaborates with other teachers as part of the literacy team.

Expected reaction to looking at student work: Positive

Focus: Variety of work

The Scenario. You stop in to talk with Mr. Z during one of his free periods one day. He begins to tell you about one student, Ryan, who

Figure 20. Follow-Up Coaching Note

Dear Ms. M:

It was great to talk to you today about your students' written responses to a reading comprehension question. Today, we looked at your top group's responses to the questions and discussed the strengths and challenge points for your students. We did a quick sort and then looked for trends in the writing of this top group. We noted that, generally, the students were able to understand the literal elements of the story but had difficulty with making inferences about the story. We talked about some of the ways that we could help this group (and the others) learn how to go beyond the text and bring their own thoughts and ideas to answering the question. It was great working with you. I will be in contact with you about doing a demonstration lesson in your class about inferences. Please let me know how the students respond to the feedback session in small groups.

Talk to you soon,
Your LC

particularly concerns him. Ryan has been held back in third grade but is still struggling with both reading and writing, and Mr. Z is wondering if he should refer Ryan to the counselor for testing. Mr. Z asks you to meet with him and another fourth-grade teacher, Ms. P, during their grade-level meeting time to help think of ways to support Ryan.

Preparing. Before the meeting, you send a note to Mr. Z, for samples of Ryan's work. You offer suggestions on what type he might include for the meeting. Before the group convenes, you look through the work and gather up a few resources that you think Mr. Z might find helpful. You also make copies of Ryan's work in addition to the ISAM protocol and send Ms. P and Mr. Z a copy so that they can become familiarized with the process (see Figure 21).

Meeting. You decide to use the ISAM Protocol (see Appendix B), and you give Mr. Z and Ms. P a copy before the meeting so they can look over the steps. When you arrive at the grade-level team meeting, you make sure to quickly state the purpose of your meeting and the use of the protocol. You start by asking Mr. Z to describe Ryan as a learner. As you begin the

Figure 21. Letter to Teacher About Meeting

Dear Mr. Z:

Thank you for bringing Ryan to my attention. For our meeting, I would like to get to know Ryan as a learner and help you set measurable goals to analyze his progress. In order to facilitate this process, can you please bring some samples of Ryan's work?

This may include:

- Journals
- Fluency records
- Running records
- Developmental spelling
- Notes
- Short-answer comprehension questions
- Essays (other types of writing)

We will be using a protocol to help analyze his work.—I have attached a copy of the steps for your review. Let me know if you have any questions. See you on Friday at 10:30.

Your LC

---

process, you jot down what he has said on large chart paper so that all three of you can look at the information together.

As you proceed, you detail what type of formative data you will be looking at as a group and write this in the first boxes of the ISAM form under formative assessment type. Next, the team spends some time looking through the work individually and noting strengths and challenges. As you go through it, you begin to form an impression of the learner.

You lead the group to the next step to discuss what they have noted. This part of the protocol is crucial and often times difficult to follow. You have noticed that it is often the case that teachers will make judgments without supporting their observations with evidence. Although it is sometimes even uncomfortable, you remind the team to back up what they have noted with examples from the work.

As you listen, an image of a particular learner begins to appear. It is obvious that Ryan is struggling to keep up in literacy. According to the running record Mr. Z has brought with him, Ryan is reading on a mid–first-grade level. The team, during their analysis, has noted that he lacks the ability to recognize certain simple sight words and that when he doesn't know a word he guesses using only the first letter to determine what the word might be. Ms. P points out the following sentence from the running record to support this observation: "The big truck stopped in the road" became "The brown truck stopped in the riding." "Sometimes," Ms. P continues, "it looks like his guesses make sense with the meaning of the sentence or passage, but often it is the case they do not." Next you begin to discuss Ryan's strengths and challenge areas during independent reading. Mr. Z provides some of his informal notes (see Figure 22).

Figure 22. Teacher's Notes About Student

Ryan—10/9
- Says he hates reading—I ask why. Changes to he only likes reading about animal and adventure stories.
- I read aloud from his book and ask deeper level inferential questions—What do you think will happen next? Why? Do you think the character was a good friend? Able to answer both with support.
- Difficulty decoding text. Sight words? Ph– sound? Ing? Stumbles many times through text—need lower level text?

Ryan says he "hates reading and writing" except books about "football." They also learn from Mr. Z's notes that Ryan is able to answer deeper level comprehension questions when the text is read aloud to him. Mr. Z confirms that Ryan's listening comprehension is very good. However, when it comes to independent reading, he spends most of the time talking, looking for new books, or "spacing out." Mr. Z has noted that during writing time, even after being told that spelling doesn't count, Ryan sometimes refuses to write because of his spelling difficulties.

As you look through one of Ryan's developmental spelling tests (see Figure 23), you can see that Ryan struggles to spell words correctly. At

Figure 23. Developmental Spelling List

#	Ryan's spelling	Correct word
1.	fan	
2.	pot	pet
3.	bag	Dig
4.	rod	rob
5.	hoop	hope
6.	wae	twait
7.	gun	gun
8.	slad	sled
9.	sick	stick
10.	shion	shine
11.	grem	dream
12.	blod	blade
13.	caoch	coach
14.	foght	fright
15.	cheriog	chewing
16.	Chall	crow
17.	wiasn	wish
18.	toen	thorn
19.	start	shouted
20.	soeit	spoil
21.	grew	growl
22.	theird	third
23.	coept	camped
24.	trys	tries
25.	chin	clapping
26.	rilnen	riding

89

first, the team only notes the problems Ryan has: reversals, short vowels, long vowels, and vowel blends. You encourage them to also see the part of words he does know how to spell correctly: beginning sounds, ending sounds, consonant blends, and sometimes consonant diagraphs. When analyzing work, it is important to note not only areas where students are lacking but also what they can do effectively because oftentimes starting with what a student does know can lead you to determine how to help in his or her learning. Mr. Z eventually decides he will use a reading inventory to interview Ryan about his reading ideas.

You look at your watch and realize time is running short. You know the next steps are crucial to helping Ryan progress. You move on to the next section: progress monitoring. Mr. Z decides to continue to assess Ryan's reading through running records and another developmental spelling list at the end of the quarter.

The team begins to set goals for Ryan. This is always one of the hardest parts of the protocol because it is difficult to know what is appropriate. You remind Mr. Z that this is a goal so that you can measure progress and the effectiveness of instruction. After much discussion, the team decides that they would like to see Ryan move up at least one level based on his running records and also to show improvement in his word knowledge, which is measured by spelling more words correctly as determined by the developmental spelling test in the next six weeks. In addition, you encourage Mr. Z to notice whether Ryan is using other strategies besides just determining a word by its first letter.

As a group, the team discusses ways to help support Ryan's learning. To help Ryan with sight words, Mr. Z will create a group of sight words on index cards so that Ryan can practice words both in and out of class. During independent reading time, Ryan will be allowed to look through some of his favorite books (no matter the level), in addition to having some books to read and understand on his level. Mr. Z will share with Ryan his running record and his goals for the next six weeks. While Mr. Z is concerned about telling Ryan that he is below grade level in his reading, you remind him that he should also share Ryan's strengths in listening comprehension. Finally, Mr. Z has decided that several students in his class will benefit by a variety of word-solving strategies. He and Ms. P have decided to create similar anchor charts, which remind students about ways to determine an unknown word. Finally, to address Ryan's spelling,

Mr. Z will work on explicitly teaching Ryan short and long vowels through a variety of hands-on activities.

Follow-Up. The meeting is over. Before you leave, you offer to observe Ryan in class over the next few days to get to know him better. Mr. Z invites you to come in on Wednesday at 9:00 a.m. to watch him during independent reading time and note his behaviors. You agree. As you are leaving, Ms. P mentions that she would love to talk to you about one of her students, Daniella, who is having similar problems. You tell her you will send her a note to set up a time to meet.

While thinking about these scenarios may be overwhelming at first, it is the practice with various protocols and interactions with teachers that will make this aspect of coaching more fluid. One can see why it is imperative to build relationships with teachers and to build a culture of looking at student work collaboratively through the formative coaching cycle.

REFLECTING AND EXTENDING

Chapter 3 examined specific techniques for making sense of student work with the underlying principle that teaching, as well as coaching, needs to be differentiated. As you begin to look through formative data, it will become clear that the best learning environment is one that responds to the needs of the learners. Becoming acquainted with students' strengths and challenge areas will help teachers prepare lessons that propel learners' literacy instruction forward. Your choice of protocols will depend on the goal of the meeting and the type of data you have available. Although using a highly structured protocol may not fit every coaching circumstance, there are benefits to using such a format. However, depending on the teacher, coach, and context of your meeting, you can differentiate your approach to make sense of student work.

QUESTIONS TO CONSIDER

1. Can you think of a time when you differentiated your coaching? Explain this situation.

2. Describe a classroom where the teacher successfully differentiated the instruction. What systems/routines did the teacher have that helped to tailor the instruction? What data did he or she use to differentiate the teaching?

3. Gather a sample of student work. Use one of the protocols to analyze the data. How did this approach work for you? What parts where you comfortable with? What parts were challenging for you? How might you do this differently next time?

CHAPTER 4

Batter Up!

Imagine This!

In an effort to get to know the teaching staff, you decide to eat lunch in the teachers' lounge. You casually join a conversation two teachers are having about the best way to teach students to develop and note questions they have about a text. You enthusiastically add some of your own thoughts, and one of the teachers seems interested. You make a plan to meet with her to talk after school one day. Remembering what you have learned about formative coaching, you ask her if she has any work that the students have done that you can look at together. As you use the quick sort protocol (see Chapter 3 and Appendix B) you realize that students are asking literal questions. You have a great idea for how you can help.

You jump at the opportunity and offer to demonstrate a lesson on questioning in her class. She eagerly accepts, and you arrange a time to meet with her before the lesson to discuss the content and details of the plan. You agree on a date and time, and at that time you go to her class with chart paper and markers in hand. You have worked all night to refine your innovative lesson that will help the students understand how to form questions.

When you arrive in her classroom the next morning, she introduces you to the students and tells them what they will be learning. She seems happy to have you in the classroom to model the lesson. Excited, you happily go to stick your chart paper on the board to begin teaching. You turn around and notice the teacher standing at the door of the classroom with papers in hand. She smiles sweetly to you and calls out, "I'll be back in a little while. I'm sure they'll have it down by then. Do you want me to get you some coffee while I'm gone?" You look at her, dumbfounded, and say, "No, thank you." It is time to begin to model your lesson. Somehow, along the path to becoming a literacy coach, you have found yourself in the role of a substitute teacher.

Wouldn't it be nice if coaching came with a game board that was clearly marked with a start and finish point and directions to help you on the path? We could all gather our game pieces, toss the dice, and we would be on our way. But for most coaches, the fact is, the game keeps changing. New players rotate in and out, wild cards are thrown every turn, and what it takes to win keeps changing.

Perhaps you have followed the rules: you have worked on forming relationships and even begun to meet with teachers about student work. Your work has been spent analyzing formative data with teachers and identifying goals for learning. But where do you go from here?

The Role and Qualifications of the Reading Coach in the United States (International Reading Association, 2004) lists various coaching activities and levels of intensity for different types of coaching (see Table 14). Most of your activities as you begin your role as the literacy coach probably have fallen into Level 1 and Level 2. While you have progressed through the formative analysis cycle, you have worked on forming relationships with teams and being seen as a resource for your colleagues. At the same time, you have met with teachers, analyzed assessments, and even planned lessons collaboratively. Now it is time to move to Level 3 of your coaching.

Level 3 activities can be the most difficult because they engender the need for trust and risk-taking from both parties. As the coach, you may have made recommendations based on the work the teacher has shared. Now it is the time to support the teacher in his or her classroom. This may mean modeling or coteaching a lesson. It may mean collecting student work or reflecting about the effectiveness of a particular instructional technique. All of these Level 3 activities involve collaboration and

Table 14. Coaching Activities and Levels of Intensity

Level 1	Level 2	Level 3
• Conversations with colleagues • Developing and providing materials for/with colleagues • Developing curriculum with colleagues	• Coplanning lessons • Holding team meetings • Interpreting assessment data	• Modeling and discussing lessons • Coteaching lessons • Analyzing videotaped lessons of teachers

vulnerability as both teacher and coach expose themselves to honest feedback about their instruction.

As you look through the student work, you will naturally begin to ask the question, "So now what?" Working alongside the teacher, you have analyzed a formative assessment. From the data, it appears some of the students are achieving, while others are not. Where do you go from here? Unfortunately, this is where many teachers and coaches get frustrated. While both parties may be able to identify strengths and weaknesses in their learners, knowing what the next steps should be to help the students is difficult.

As a coach, you will need to have an arsenal of teaching techniques, resources, and formative assessments to share with teachers to assist them in planning their lessons. Furthermore, you will need to know which of these supports will best assist the teacher. As you begin to plan instruction based on the needs of student, you should develop systems to make sure your time and the teacher's time is spent effectively. Even the simplest support, such as handing out resources, requires a system to be effective.

In this chapter, we look at how you can support teachers as they begin to plan instruction based on their students' needs. We examine primarily Level 2 and 3 coaching activities and focus in on systems to set up collaborative teaching environments, techniques to collect classroom formative data, and honest ways to provide feedback that encourage reflection. We investigate situations where formative data is not simply test scores but, rather, classroom observations, journals, fluency reads, and other less formalized assessments of learning. The systems you set up are integral to avoiding the slippery slope of becoming either a substitute teacher while modeling or an "evaluator" of teaching while observing a class.

Gathering Multiple Types of Data

Sometimes, as you meet with teachers to look at student work, new questions may arise that the work itself cannot answer. Looking at a piece of writing that the students didn't complete, you may wonder, What were that student's experiences during class time? How much time did he or she spend on task? What techniques did the teacher use to help keep the student focused? Did the boys participate more often than the girls? Where was the teacher positioned in the room? Did her presence make a difference in terms of student performance on the formative assessment? Although this information is often more difficult to collect than actual pieces of student work, it can be extremely valuable in helping to understand student achievement. Collecting classroom data usually takes two people: one who can keep his or her attention focused on teaching the lesson and another who can focus on collecting the data. Depending on the purpose, as a coach you can support the teacher by assuming either role.

We do not advise starting with classroom data until you have a professional relationship established with the teacher with whom you are going to work. Having someone that you do not know well collecting data can be intimidating. Usually, observation is most closely paired with the process that principals use to evaluate and rate teachers, but for formative coaching, observation is merely a part of the data collection process and not intended for evaluative purposes. In some situations, the coach might collect data as the teacher teaches the lesson; while in others, the teacher might be the one to gather data as the coach teaches. Still other situations might call for both teacher and coach to collect data and then compare their findings. As you progress through the formative coaching cycle, there may be times when you want to use observational classroom data as your formative assessment. In these instances, you would follow the same process: determine the goal for learning, identify a formative assessment, plan/teach the lesson, analyze the data to determine your next steps, and provide feedback to students. It is often most helpful to analyze observational classroom data in conjunction with the work students produced. Matching these two data sources can give you insight into student performance.

Introducing Data Collection Tools

Observational classroom data tools are ways to make meaning from the talk, actions, and environment of a classroom. This time, the data you use to support the formative data analysis cycle consist of observational notes or checklists. No matter the type of observational tools, you will still follow the path of the formative analysis cycle by choosing a goal and identifying data that you will analyze. However, taking a few extra steps before you go in to observe may be helpful in collecting the data. For example, sometimes it is a good idea to obtain a seating chart so that you can identify students by their location or predetermine where you will be located during the observation.

Beginning data collection involves discussing with the teacher the ideas or challenges he or she faces. As teachers begin to form a focus question in their heads, you can start to think of different data types that might help you understand student performance. For example, a teacher who feels that she doesn't have enough time in the day to fit in all the activities she wants might benefit from your recording how class time is actually spent. Using a time chart may allow her to see in an objective fashion how time was used during the class period. If a teacher sees that much of the time is allocated to explaining routines or procedures, it may lead to an insight about her instruction. Perhaps spending time up front to do a whole-group practice of routines for a period of time will lead to less wasted time during group time. Sometimes the data you might collect comes in the form of a checklist, while other times it might be more descriptive and based on an interview or notes about students.

Another teacher may be concerned that students are not actually reading books during their quiet reading time. Perhaps you go to the classroom and watch a few lessons and notice that some students are, in fact, not reading. You may have ideas as to why students are not reading, but before you jump to any conclusions, it's best to collect data. What kind of data can you collect that would be helpful? You may start by noticing which students look like they are reading and which do not. It may be that out of a class of 25 students, 5 of the students do not "look" like they are reading. Of course the question remains, how do you know the other 20 are actually reading independently?

Beginning this process with teachers first involves them deciding on a focus question for your classroom data collection. Talk with the teacher about the data that you could collect to help determine this. In the example above, perhaps conferencing with the students and taking notes on their discussion of the book or looking at their reading journals might allow you to understand which students are reading and which are not. It may also give you insight into why students are not reading. Maybe the books the students are reading are too hard or there is no accountability built into the lesson. As you begin to walk through the data with the teacher, you can brainstorm ideas about how to improve the lesson. As the teacher tries new ideas, you can continue to collect data and discuss what you see. Often this builds opportunities for coteaching and planning a lesson.

Once again, starting from data allows teachers to investigate their lessons and dig deeply into their instructional decisions. As you approach them with ideas and techniques, the mentoring process will seem less arbitrary and more clearly focused.

Before determining what type of data you should be collecting, it is necessary to sit down and have a conversation with the teacher. The question the teacher has will arise as he or she begins to look at the students' work and classroom performance. For some teachers, the question might come quickly, while others may not be sure what to ask. By asking the teacher a variety of questions during your conference, the focus and the question will become clearer (see Table 15). Sometimes you will find that teachers will ask a very broad question that needs to be reshaped or narrowed. Coaching them through the process of forming a question may take time but is ultimately worthwhile.

As you begin your data collection, it is important to maintain an undivided focus and to tune out the other distractions in the classroom. Your familiarity with students and the teacher will make it easier to provide feedback, which can encourage a teacher's self-reflection.

Techniques for Collecting Data

Once you decide on the focus of your data, you may want to think about what tools you might need to collect this information. The most common way of collecting data is with a paper and pencil. However, the type of instrument you use depends on what type of information you want to analyze. Using video can be a great way of looking at and reflecting on teaching or student talk after a lesson is finished.

In the following sections, we present and discuss the following data collection tools:

- Scripting: Writing down all the "talk" (student and teacher) that you hear in a classroom

Table 15. Questions to Aid in the Selection of the Appropriate Data Collection Tools

Examples of conference questions	Teacher focus question	Checklist/observational notes
Questions about encouraging independence in classroom: What types of strategies are you working on with your class?	Do students use strategies I am teaching them independently?	• Checklist of the number of times students solicit help from teacher or other students • Selective scripting of classroom talk
Questions about which students struggle: Which students struggle with ___? How do you know? Which students are you most concerned about? Why?	Are my lower-level students better able to work independently or collaboratively on X skill?	• Checklist of students who have difficulty getting started with an activity • Time-on-task tracker • Observational notes/checklist of how students spend class time, noting student behaviors periodically through lesson • Interview with students who do not complete activity about what they found difficult
Questions about timing: Do you struggle with fitting everything into the day? Where do you think you lose time? Do you feel that certain groups/individuals require more of your time than others? How do you feel transitions work in your classroom?	Which students do I spend the most time working with? Where does the time go during my class period? How do students ask for help?	• Time allotment chart • Time-on-task tracker • Number of interruptions chart

- Feedback monitoring: Noting the type of feedback students receive about their work throughout a lesson
- Activity tracker: Noting the varying types of activities that teachers and students engage in during class time
- Time on task: Noting the specific amount of time that individual or groups of students focus on a task

- Interviewing: A one-on-one conference with a student in order to gain insight into the student's understanding

As you read about these techniques for collecting data, it is beneficial to picture what observations might help bring more clarity to the teachers' work in your own school. Which teachers with whom you work might gain further insight into curriculum and instruction?

Scripting

Scripting is a term for recording what you hear spoken in a class. When you script, you write down the talk that you hear in a classroom. Selective scripting is a closely related technique where only select dialogue is tracked. You might choose to script only the conversation of a certain group of learners in order to learn more about those particular individuals, or you might use selective scripting to record a distinct part of the lesson.

Scripting can be used to collect data about an individual classroom or a school as a whole (see Appendix A for the Scripting Tool and the Types of Talk Tool). To collect this information, you will again want to determine a focus before you start. Because there is so much conversation in a classroom, you should decide on what you want to record. Will you write down everything you hear or will you perhaps use selective scripting to record the talk of a specific group of students? The answer to which path to pursue is determined by the teacher's focus. Consider the example of Ms. H, a first-grade teacher. Ms. H has noticed that students are having trouble answering higher order thinking questions. She says they are having problems drawing simple conclusions, and she is not sure why. She has come to you to ask your advice. You decide together that you will use a selective scripting device called question monitoring. This tool simply focuses your scripting on the type of questions that are asked. You and the teacher decide on this observational technique because you both are wondering how much practice students receive with higher order thinking questions.

As you look through a "script" with a teacher (for example, see Figure 24), you may notice themes or find trends. These may lead to new ideas about effective instruction. In this example, the teacher wants to know if she is asking enough higher order questions. Without passing judgment,

Figure 24. Sample of Scripting

Focus: Teacher's questions
Time: 10:10–10:20 (Whole-class instruction)
Teacher: Ms. H
Grade: 3

Start time: 10:10

- What did we cover yesterday?
- What does *predict* mean?
- Right, and who else predicts?
- [Starts reading text]
- Okay, where did we leave off?
- What happened the other day?
- Who was the new character introduced?
- What type of animal is he?
- What is the problem that he has?
- Where does he go?
- What do you think he is going to do next?
- Why did he steal the cheese?
- Do you think the farmer will notice?
- What clues do you think he will use to solve the mystery?

End time: 10:20

you can simply show her that in 10 minutes, she asked 14 questions. Out of those questions, the teacher may conclude that only three can be considered higher order questions that require students to go beyond what is written in the text. Also, as you review the script with the teacher, you may notice that the teacher does not ask students to explain their thinking. She is simply satisfied with an answer. Only in the last question does she ask students to identify textual evidence to support their answer. Scripting allows the teacher to be aware of and have a record of her own teaching. Of course, you might look at the same lesson and choose to use instead a verbal tracking tool, which records who is doing the talking and what is being asked. For example, you might notice that the same four children are the only ones who participate in the lesson. Or maybe as you look through responses, students do not support their ideas with textual evidence. It is often the case that you may follow a classroom observation with another soon after in order to gather more evidence.

Feedback Monitoring

Tracking the feedback students receive throughout a lesson takes careful observation. Sometimes, feedback is received verbally, but often teachers give nonverbal clues. Additionally, there are other sources of feedback such as peers and self-evaluation or self-reflection. When tracking feedback in the classroom, you may note what type of feedback is given, by whom, how often, and if it is positive or negative. Depending on the goal of the observation, you might want to note students' reactions to the feedback.

Ms. W approaches you one day and wonders why her students' responses to their reading lack any depth. Although they summarize the information they have read, they do not go deeply into the story and add any of their own thoughts. Ms. W has talked about this to her students, but it has made no difference. When you discuss feedback with her, Ms. W explains that she gives her students a grade for their journal entry based on a rubric that she has developed and stapled into their notebook and that she, in addition, writes her own letter back to the students. Ms. W is interested in collecting data on how students respond to her feedback. She asks that you observe in the classroom as she hands back the journals and interview a few of her students about their responses. The next day, when you observe, you notice that Ms. W. hands back the journals, but then gives no time for students to read her comments. While she verbally praises one student for his "deep interpretations" in his writing, she does not provide any models for this for the other students. Afterwards, you pull a few students in the class to talk to them. The students agree that they rarely read Ms. W's comments, and if they do, they mostly forget what she has written by the time they begin their next journal entry. They say it probably would be helpful to have a reminder to go back and read the comments before they start their next entry.

You meet with Ms. W and share the results. You both decide to (1) give students time to read the comments in class, (2) have students underline the two most important comments from Ms. W's responses to them before they start writing, and (3) have Ms. W make overhead copies of entries that are showing the deeper-level thinking she would like to see in the journals and keep them posted in the room. In this way, Ms. W will be providing feedback to them that is both visual and auditory. They will also be reminded to go back and look at her particular suggestions and comments before they begin to write again.

Activity Tracker

Sometimes noting what teachers and students actually do during the lesson period will shed light on next steps. Of course a lesson plan may help detail student and teacher activities, but lesson plans often change in the classroom. Again, the way you track student or teacher activity will depend on your purpose.

Take the example of Mr. F, who feels that his eighth-grade students are disengaged throughout the period. Although they are well behaved, there seems to be little enthusiasm or energy from the students. Mr. F seems to do most of the talking and thinking in the class. You decide to track student and teacher activities by noting what both are doing at predetermined intervals. After looking through your observational notes, you notice that throughout the 90-minute block, students spend most of the time reading aloud or verbally answering questions. You have also tracked the teacher's movements throughout the class. He stays seated at the front throughout the lesson, only getting up at one interval to move to write something on the board.

As you review this data with the teacher, he becomes aware that his activity and students' energy are related. You suggest some simple techniques for engaging the class by encouraging Mr. F to move around the room. You also work with him to develop learning activities that give students the opportunity for collaborative and creative thinking and that incorporate activities for kinesthetic and visual learners.

Time on Task

The chart in Figure 25 shows an example of a data collection tool to gather information about students' on- and off-task behavior throughout their independent reading lesson. It is helpful before arriving in a teacher's classroom to have a seating chart. You may also want to determine where you will be located or if you will move around throughout the lesson to collect data. In the instance described in Figure 25, you may decide with the teacher to collect data at three different predetermined times throughout the lesson. It is important to create clear definitions for what

Figure 25. Sample of Time-on-Task Device

	Time Interval 1 10:00	Time Interval 2 10:20	Description of behavior
Activity	10:00 = Independent reading	10:20 = Journal writing	
Total number of students = 20	On task: 15 Off task: 5	On task: 10 Off task: 10	
Target student: David	Off task Reading *Tales of a Fourth Grade Nothing* Talking to neighbor	Off task Flipping through book Using book as fan Looking out window Sharpens pencil	Time 1: Talking to neighbor—5 mins—Teacher calls David's name...goes back to reading Time 2: 10 minutes
Target student: Melissa	On task Reading *Scorpions*	Off task Looking for notebook	Time 1: Seems engaged—doesn't look up from book during observation Time 2: Gets up out of seat Tears out paper Crumples paper

you are observing. In this example, the teacher defines on-task behavior as either demonstrating reading behavior or writing in their journals. Recognize that data collection on this level can be very challenging and requires the ability to attend to many different things at once.

In Figure 25, the literacy coach chose two time intervals to collect data about the students: 10:00 and 10:20. At these times, the coach counted the number of students that are on and off task. Then she observed a few target students identified by the teacher to use as examples of what students are doing during the lesson. This data can then be shared with the teacher.

It may be that the teacher is not aware of when the students are on and off task because of all the other items she must attend to throughout the lesson. From Figure 25, you can see that the students lose focus during the writing portion of the lesson. This naturally leads to questions and a coaching conversation about why this occurs. Did students need more structure for the journal writing? How can the transition between the activities run more smoothly? What is the goal behind the journal writing? How were students held accountable? Looking at the data collected for the target students may help the classroom teacher prevent students from going off task by taking simple actions such as making sure there are sharpened pencils or notebooks easily accessible.

For the same lesson, the teacher might want to collect data by doing an interview or providing a few students with a survey about their reading. For example, the teacher may decide to briefly interview a few students who are struggling during independent reading time while the coach teaches a lesson. This interview might be conducted either orally or in writing, depending on the proficiency of the readers. After reviewing the notes from the interview, it might be clear that some students have chosen books that are too difficult and cannot read many words on the page. This, in turn, has contributed to off-task behavior. The teacher might then choose to monitor the books students are reading by doing weekly fluency checks and develop lesson plans to help with decoding multisyllabic words.

Interviewing

One of the simplest ways of collecting data is to take the time to talk to a student and try and understand the student's thinking. Teachers often do not have the time to do this because of the needs of the other students in the class. As a coach, you have the ability to listen closely to individual students or to provide teachers with the opportunity to do so without the other distractions of teaching. One of the most important and useful ways we have collected data is to have students provide insight into their thinking.

Within Ms. B's third-grade class, it became clear that although students could explain the difference between fact and opinion, they were having trouble applying it. As the literacy coach and Ms. B review some fact and opinion questions, they notice that students seemed to almost haphazardly pick the answer.

The coach follows up by interviewing the students to learn more about their understanding of fact and opinion. Ms. B recommends four students for the coach to interview. As the coach discusses fact and opinion with the students, she notices that students define fact as something that they all believe is true. Therefore, when students are given a statement about an opinion that they all share, they automatically feel that this is fact. When they hear the statement about their favorite singer "Ashanti is a great singer," they consider this a fact because everyone they know agrees with them. As the literacy coach learns more about the nuances of their understanding, she shares this with the teacher who then uses this and similar examples in her next lessons.

The Power of Collaborative Teaching: Strategies for Meaningful Collaboration

Often you will find yourself excited about the possibilities of a particular teaching strategy that affects student learning. You might think to yourself that if teachers used this strategy more often, student literacy achievement could truly grow. Some of the best tools you have in helping teachers to incorporate new teaching strategies are demonstration, coteaching, and providing meaningful feedback. It is your presence in the classroom that will help teachers find the support they need to take risks and try something new.

Modeling Versus Demonstrating

There is something that makes people nervous when they hear the word *modeling*. Perhaps it harkens back to the image of a supermodel, airbrushed and flawless, strolling down the catwalk, wearing the latest trend while an applauding crowd secretly searches for evidence of cellulite. The audience never knows or cares about the hours the model has spent in the gym, the careful choices she has made to further her career, or her own feelings about how the show went. The audience expects perfection. The model, herself, becomes a performance.

When we talk about a coach teaching a lesson in another person's classroom, we like to use the term *demonstration lesson*. The role of the coach is not to show an airbrushed version of a lesson but rather to roll up her sleeves and demonstrate the gritty aspects of teaching a lesson, including planning, teaching, preparing, and reflecting. So, too, the teacher's role moves from being an adoring or critical audience member to an active participant in the demonstration. Because demonstration lessons are perhaps one of the most important ways to support teachers, it is important to set clear expectations of all parties involved.

It can be difficult to teach in someone else's classroom with someone else's students, but demonstration is integral to the success of coaching. Although knowing and espousing theory and research is important, it is feedback and in-class coaching that actually leads to the transfer of newly learned skills. Joyce and Showers (1995) point out that it takes 20–25 trials in classrooms before a new teaching technique becomes part of a teacher's repertoire. Teachers need to see examples of how a new teaching strategy might look in their own classroom setting before trying it themselves. Seeing a technique demonstrated in their own classroom allows them to create a visual picture of how they might go about trying it. It is the practice of skills in their own classroom that leads to the acquisition of new understanding (Dole, 2004). Steps to guide the modeling process are provided in Table 16 and are discussed in detail in the sections that follow.

Before the Demonstration Lesson. As excited as you may be to have been invited into someone's classroom to teach a lesson, make sure that before you go into a classroom to model, you discuss expectations. If left undone, the teacher may see the time in the class as nothing more than

Table 16. Steps of the Demonstration Process

Before demonstrating a lesson, ask	During demonstration	After demonstrating a lesson
What would you like me to model? How will this fit into your curriculum?	Make sure you have all the materials you will need.	Meet with the teacher and do a reflective think-aloud of the lesson.
[Observe the teacher and students in the classroom.]	Focus on the students, not the teacher.	Ask for what the teacher noticed.
Are there any students who present special challenges?	Involve the teacher.	Discuss follow-up activities and/or future plans for modeling or collaborating on a lesson.
What will you be doing while I model the lesson?	Be aware of time.	
Can I share some of the choices I have made? Do you have any feedback?	Have high expectations for students.	Consider and analyze student work.
[Prepare all the materials you will need.]	Use best instructional practices.	

an extra free period. Think back to the vignette at the beginning of the chapter, which was an actual scenario we have experienced as literacy coaches. Although there was an initial conference with the teacher, there wasn't a clear conversation about the role of the teacher during the demonstration lesson. In addition, the link to student work wasn't apparent or discussed. In retrospect, the coach could have suggested that the teacher look at the work or responses of the students during the lesson and make a formative assessment of their understanding. The coach might have also made plans to follow up and to discuss both the student work after the lesson and how the instructional strategies supported the evidence of student learning. Having clear expectations before the modeling will help to facilitate a meaningful conversation centered on student needs.

Even if the teacher will only be observing you, take time to discuss what he or she will watch for in your lesson. What will the teacher write down? How does the teacher plan to use these notes? Setting a clear expectation creates a professional tone for the observation and should prevent teachers from viewing this as an extra free period. Once you have decided on a lesson, make sure that you have fully planned it out. Remember that you are demonstrating best practice, so arriving fully prepared to the lesson is extremely important. Bring all the materials you will need. If you have a written lesson plan, let the teacher see it prior to the lesson. The teacher's knowledge of the students may help you develop the plan.

Consider this scenario. You made a quick stop to check in with Ms. W, a new teacher. She mentioned to you that her students have been struggling with questioning skills. She has asked you to demonstrate a lesson on questioning for her. Although you both are very busy, you schedule a meeting during the only time she is available—10 minutes before the students enter. You know she will be distracted and you will have very little time to meet with her. It's important to use your time wisely. But how do you conduct this meeting efficiently so that both of you can prepare for your lesson?

Asking the following questions can help you and the teacher get the most out of the demonstration session.

- What do you want to see me demonstrate? What standard does this align with? How does this fit into your curriculum?

- What should I know about the students in your classroom? Are there any particular students of whom I should be made aware or differentiate for when preparing my lesson?
- How will you follow up on this lesson? How do you want me to follow up on it?
- What kind of data will you collect as I am teaching that will help you?

If you have no time to meet with the teacher beforehand, you can e-mail the teacher the Collaboration Planner and have her complete it and send it back to you (see Figure 26 for a sample, and see Appendix A for a reproducible template). This collaboration template is a way of making explicit the goal of the lesson and the roles that both teacher and coach will play during this time. It can be used whether you are coteaching or demonstrating a lesson. During the initial discussion, Ms. W explains that she has decided to have her students practice forming questions about a variety of texts. She wants students to be able to do this so that they can become active readers and participate in book groups, which she plans to start in the next few weeks. During this first meeting, you make it a point to find out what the students have already been exposed to and if there are any individuals who may require extra attention. Coaching often requires demonstrating lessons; however, it is good protocol to inquire about any special needs that students might have. For example, a student who has grapho-motor problems may struggle needlessly through a lesson because it wasn't discussed that he has difficulty focusing on higher order cognitive skills such as questioning when he has to write with a pen and paper. Simply asking the teacher to identify students' special needs and interests will help prepare for a more effective lesson. In the example of Ms. W, the teacher has also agreed to observe the lesson and write down questions that two of the groups create. In this way, the literacy coach has let the teacher know that she is also an active participant in the lesson.

During the Demonstration. Even though you are aware of someone watching you during the lesson, the focus is still primarily on the students. Although it may be tempting to comment on a lesson or explain why you have done something as the lesson unfolds, try to resist the temptation. The situation should mimic a real classroom situation, and it should be focused on the students in front of you. So as not to add to the confusion of the students, use the teacher's routines and structures as much as possible. As with all good lesson plans, it is extremely important that you make the

Figure 26. Sample Collaboration Planner

Type of support: Demonstration lesson Class: Ms. W—fourth grade Date: April 17, 2008 Time: Fifth period	
Focus of the lesson Forming open-ended questions	Materials needed Chart paper (Ms. W provides) Markers (Ms. W provides)
Formative information to collect/observe Students' questions	Role of coach Demonstration lesson on questioning
Role of teacher Ms. W has decided to observe and write down how I model questioning for students and then the questions formed by students in group A and C.	Students/groups to be made aware of John P. (front row, center)—special education student, works well with Ryan, has grapho-motor issues and uses keyboard. Students have just finished unit on nonfiction, are aware of features of nonfiction, and are very interested in literature about space.
Follow-up (teacher) Ms. W will meet with me the next day, and we will assess the questions that the students have created.	Follow-up (literacy coach) LC will meet with Ms. W to brainstorm next lessons and will return next Tuesday to observe lesson.

goal of the lesson clear to the students and think about how students with different needs will adjust to the task at hand. Finally, be aware of time and make sure that you have a few minutes to wrap up the lesson at the end.

After Demonstrating a Lesson. As soon as possible, arrange to meet with the teacher to discuss the lesson. There are many ways to conduct this postdemonstration session. For instance, you may want to do a lesson think-aloud, where you model reflective thinking about your own lesson. Some questions to inform your think-aloud are as follows:

- How did you decide on the plan? How did you decide on the activity?
- What were you noticing while you were teaching? What questions did you have?
- Were there any particular students who stood out during the lesson? Why?
- What kind of "at a glance" formative data were you using? What kinds of deeper-level data do you think you could use to analyze student understanding?
- What would you change about your lesson? Why?
- What are the next steps?

The following vignette illustrates what a think-aloud might look like.

***

So, let me walk you through my lesson plan so that you can understand my thinking. I wanted to start the lesson with a hook to capture their attention. I thought through a number of ideas and decided on having a small activity where they chose an open-ended question out of a bag and asked their neighbor a question. This was just to get the lesson started. The kids seemed to really like this activity, but it took longer than I had wanted. Still, I think it started the lesson off on the right foot, so it was worth the time.

Afterward, I introduced the lesson and told them what the day's goal was. I tried to make the goal concrete and measurable. I wanted them to be able to evaluate what they understood from the lesson. I then decided to talk to them about the difference between open-ended questions and what I called "close-ended." Rather than tell them the difference, I showed them a variety of examples of the two types of questions and asked them to think about what open-ended and close-ended meant. I had them turn and talk—a strategy that gets not just the students who raise their hands to participate but everyone. I was able to walk around and hear some of the students' ideas. They seemed right on target, so I just reviewed the terms quickly and wrote the definitions of these two terms on the chart paper. I always like to make charts to serve as reminders for students to use when they are working independently. I looked at my watch and realized I was running behind—I always feel that way.

The next step I had in mind was to read the short article on Mars and have them develop open- and close-ended questions because you told me the students were interested in learning more about space. I knew I wouldn't have enough time to get through the whole article, so instead of having them read it to themselves, I read the first two paragraphs to them. Then I showed them how I created an open-ended question based on what I read, using the chart we had created as a class to help me.

While I was doing this think-aloud, I could tell some of the students' focus was lagging. I had to find some way to engage them. So I quickly gave them a question and had them vote with a thumbs up or thumbs down if they thought it was open-ended. I called on Jennifer and asked her to explain her thinking because I wanted to know if she understood what I had been demonstrating. I only did this thumbs-up/thumbs-down part of the lesson because I could tell that some were phasing out. As you see in my lesson plan, I was going to have the students read the rest of the text independently or with a partner. However, I knew I was under a time crunch. So instead, I decided to read the text to them and then have them go back to their desk and create two open-ended questions. Originally, I was going to have them also create some close-ended questions, but I realized that this could be confusing.

Getting the students back to their desks took a while, and I started thinking about some routines you might want to try with your students to speed this process up. As the students were creating their questions, I walked around to help some of those who I thought were struggling. What I realized was that two of the questions were proving too much for some of the students and not challenging enough for others. I think this part of the lesson should have been differentiated. If I were going to do it again, I might not limit the number to two—or I might have another part of the activity that those students who were moving quickly could progress to. At the very end of the lesson, I had a few students share their questions.

Finally, I asked them to turn and talk and tell their partner what they had learned today about questions. Based on what I heard, students seemed to understand the difference between open-ended and close-ended questions.

However, now I am glad that I collected the questions because I was able to use them as formative assessment of what they understood. Looking at the questions, I could tell that three of the students were really struggling to understand the lesson both when I walked around and in their development of the written questions. I examined their questions carefully and made an initial assessment that these students were still not clear on how to form questions—they seemed limited in the words they had to create a question. I think I would review questions with them and maybe even provide them with a chart if they demonstrated the need for extra reinforcement. Also, I could tell from questioning at the end of the lesson that many students didn't seem to quite get why they needed this skill or how it would serve them in the future. If I were to do this again, I think I would want to hit this part harder. Looking at the questions, I think my next steps would be to have the students create questions based on a story they read independently. If that was successful, then I would have them begin discussions. Again, though, I would break this down into a number of steps before starting these discussion groups. I would pull a few of the students aside to review open- and close-ended questions.

The think-aloud portion of your postconference may be one of the most important parts of your meeting with the teacher, as it serves to clarify your choices and decisions. Additionally, it models the kind of thinking you would want them to do before and after teaching a lesson. As you walk through the lesson, do not be afraid to mention the challenges or activities you might do differently. You can find the Coach Planning Sheet for a Think-Aloud in Appendix A to help guide the think-aloud portion.

Asking the teacher to review the notes they took and tell you what they noticed from the lesson is also a starting point for encouraging reflective teaching. As you review the lesson, focus on how to follow up on this lesson. Will you model another lesson? Will you collaboratively look at the student work produced from this activity or coplan the next lesson? Finally, remember to thank the teacher for the time in his or her classroom.

Coteaching

As you begin to plan your next steps, you may want to consider planning and teaching a lesson together. Friend, Reising, and Cook (1993) identify five techniques for teacher collaboration that are typically used when teaching collaboratively. We have applied them to how a coach and teacher might use these to consider how they might work together.

1. Lead and support: Both teacher and coach may plan the lesson together, but the coach leads the lesson while the teacher supports or collects further formative data on students. This fits into the paradigm of the model or demonstration lesson but assigns a role for the teacher to play as well.

2. Station teaching: Students are split into groups and assigned to a work station. The coach and teacher each take responsibility for the group's learning activities at a particular station (see Figure 27). Usually, the students switch stations so that the teacher and coach see multiple groups of students.

3. Parallel teaching: Teacher and coach plan a lesson together, and each delivers the same content to a small group.

4. Alternative teaching: The teacher or coach instructs the class, while the other pulls a small group to reteach or accelerate instruction. We often do this when we want to know more about a select group of students as learners.

5. Team teaching: Both teacher and coach share the planning and teaching of a lesson. They each play a role in delivering the lesson, sharing the responsibility for teaching and learning. In Figure 28, for example, the teacher elicits students' ideas about their writing as the coach jots down their responses.

Figure 27. Station Teaching

Figure 28. Team Teaching

You can think about these models of collaboration through the perspective of the gradual release of responsibility. As you move from the lead and support model to team teaching, the responsibility of teaching begins to shift. Therefore, when considering where to start, always consider how much support the teacher needs and how much time you have to plan together. Due to the true shared nature of team teaching, it often takes the most planning as both teacher and coach go through their role in the lesson. However, sharing a lesson can be an extremely exciting way of collaborating.

For example, in our school, when we first decided to introduce the QAR model (Raphael et al., 2006), we developed a whole-school professional development session around the technique in order to demonstrate what it was and how teachers might use it in their classroom. The staff was interested but not quite sure even after a few workshops how to implement QAR with their class. In the beginning, we started by offering classroom support to various teachers. Ms. L, an experienced third-grade teacher, asked for a few demonstration lessons to be conducted in her classroom. Ms. L was interested in QAR right from the start. Gabrielle followed up with her shortly after the workshop to look at some of the ways her students had answered reading comprehension questions. It was clear that her students were not always able to identify what a particular question was asking them to do. Sometimes students would answer the question by relying only on what they previously knew about the topic, and other times they wouldn't allow their thinking to go beyond the text so that drawing a conclusion or making an inference was nearly impossible. Gabrielle started coaching by demonstrating the planning, teaching, and reflection of a few lessons. After the demonstration lessons, Ms. L and Gabrielle began to teach side by side. Sometimes, they would take small groups and sometimes share the responsibility of one 15-minute whole-group lesson.

When Ms. L started to see her students using QAR, it wasn't long until she was using this technique in all the subject areas. Excitedly she would share with Gabrielle that the students had applied QAR to answer science questions and even math. Her comfort in teaching QAR became obvious. She shared her ideas and new applications of the technique with both coaches thereafter.

Planning Your Support With the Gradual Release of Responsibility Model

Most coaches miss working with students. When given the opportunity to work with a teacher, without much forethought they quickly step right into the classroom and begin working with students. There have been many times that we have been so excited to teach a particular lesson that we have happily gone into the classroom to demonstrate it to the teacher. Maybe we spent a few days in the classroom working with the teacher and students. Yet, when we would visit a few weeks later, the classroom might be back to the way it was before the previous visit. It was like our coaching never happened. Consider the following scenario.

The coach has demonstrated to the teacher how to do think-alouds for the students by explicitly modeling reading strategies. The coach comes in for a week to model for the teacher. Although there isn't much time to talk about the lessons, the coach does a quick check-in with the teacher during lunch. "Did you get what I was doing?" she asks the teacher. "Yes, I think I can do that with my students. They seemed to really like it." For the next several weeks the coach asks the teacher if she has done think-alouds with her class. She says no, but really wants to get to it. A few months later, and the teacher still has not gotten to it yet.

What happened? The answer is simple. The coach never set up systems to support the teacher's learning. While coaches may spend hours thinking of ways to help the teacher create lessons that scaffold the students' learning until they are capable of independent application, when it comes to the teacher's learning, we often drop the ball. We hope that simply seeing a few demonstration lessons will be enough for teachers to then try it alone with their class on a different day with a different text.

You may have come across the term *gradual release of responsibility* in your own classroom teaching (Pearson & Gallagher, 1983). The gradual release of responsibility encompasses the various activities a teacher engages in with learners to build their capability to apply these skills independently in novel situations. To build this independence, teachers may meet with a small group and explicitly model a skill. Then, they may guide learners through a series of activities, allowing them to practice with a partner for support until the student is able to independently apply this skill on her own. Pearson and Gallagher's model takes into account the shift in responsibility as the learner takes on the foundation of the new skill. Keeping the gradual release model in mind while you are coaching is important so that teachers acquire the skills to be independent practitioners, able to apply and build on the instructional techniques you coach them in. Otherwise, teachers can become too reliant on you to teach a certain topic, analyze a particular type of formative assessment, or plan a lesson.

For coaching, we identify five stages of the gradual release model that decrease in the amount of support the coach provides. These stages are as follows: (1) demonstrating, (2) side by side, (3) shifting, (4) application, and (5) sharing (see Figure 29).

During the demonstration stage, the coach will spend time in the classroom, demonstrating a lesson. As the teacher becomes more comfortable, he or she may collaborate or take turns teaching. During the shifting stage, the coach and teacher make a joint decision to shift responsibility of teaching to the instructor of the class. While the coach may still help plan and teach the lesson, the responsibility moves solely to the teacher. Usually during this time, the coach checks in formally or informally with the teacher. As teachers move into the application

Figure 29. Gradual Release of Responsibility Model for Coaches

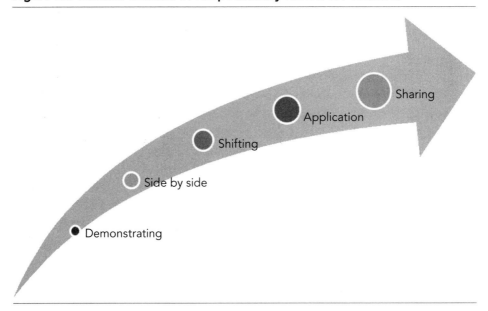

phase, they begin to feel confident with newly acquired skills and make them their own. At this point, they may feel comfortable asking for your feedback about a lesson or wanting you to collect data on various aspects of the students' engagement. During the application phase, teachers take risks by applying these newly acquired skills to novel situations. They build upon what you have showed them, adding to and changing it to suit their curriculum and, most importantly, students' needs. Finally, during the sharing phase, teachers feel ownership over their new learning and are able to share it with other members of their school. They are able to collaborate with other teachers by modeling, coplanning, or coteaching a lesson (see Table 17 for examples of the various stages of the gradual release of responsibility for coaching teachers).

The gradual release of responsibility in coaching is not always a linear process. Sometimes, you may find yourself moving toward the shifting stage and realize that the teacher may still require more support. Sometimes the release takes a long time, while in other instances the teacher may stay on the application stage without feeling confident enough to share with others. There are times when you may begin your coaching with a teacher already on the application stage, and you ask to help support her as she moves toward sharing her skills with other teachers. For each teacher, your coaching will be different, depending on the context of the situation and your relationship and knowledge about that person.

As you work with teachers, it is important to reflect on how you spend your time. Using the Record of Coaching Activities chart, like the one in Figure 30, can serve as a quick overview of whom you are coaching and how you have spent your time (see Appendix A for a reproducible version of this form). This, in essence, is another type of formative data that helps with your coaching. The coach can use this chart to think about how the activities they are using with individual teachers support the gradual release of responsibility model. Consider, for instance, the following scenario.

Ms. A sought out the coach in order to obtain recommendations for resources. Ms. A was looking for leveled texts focused on young people who were heroes, a theme she was working on with her class. When the coach located some texts and brought them to her, Ms. A expressed that she was concerned with her reading group that was far below grade level and the progress they were making. The conversation was casual

Table 17. What Coaching Looks Like During the Gradual Release of Responsibility

Stage	Description	What the coach does	What the teacher does
Demonstrating	Coach models instructional strategy	Model lesson planning, analysis of student work, utilization of formative data, specific lesson for small or large group, reflection after lesson, ways to collaborate	Observe; gather data; ask questions; offer suggestions about students, resources, or lessons; videotape lesson; discuss lesson with grade-level group or other team
Side by side	Coach and teacher may analyze, plan and teach together; responsibility of the formative analysis cycle is shared	Offer guidance in the form of resources, reminders, feedback, suggestions; can provide the teacher an opportunity to focus on a smaller group of students or practice a new skill (by coteaching)	Plan, teach, or analyze data with the support of the coach
Shifting	Coach and teacher make a joint decision to shift responsibility of teaching to the instructor of the class	May still help plan and teach lesson (usually over a period of time); provide feedback to teacher from observations of student learning	Takes major responsibility of planning, teaching, and implementing lesson
Application	Teacher takes responsibility for instructional strategy and builds on skills	Checks in periodically with teacher; may collect further formative data; provide feedback to teacher from observations of student learning	Applies newly acquired skills to novel situations, feels confident taking risks, may conduct action research based on newly acquired skills
Sharing	Teacher feels confident in her ability to share newly learned information with other teachers	Set up opportunities for peer observation and mentoring so that others can see how technique is used in the classroom	May facilitate professional development workshops and have teachers visit in her classroom to learn about this instructionally strategy

Figure 30. Sample Record of Coaching Activities

Name of teacher	10/1	10/2	10/3	10/4	10/5	10/8	10/9	10/10	10/11
Ms. A	R		AF	Obs		AF/LP	LP	D	Me/CT
Ms. R					CI	R			
Mr. W	LP	D	LP	CT					
Ms. D	TS	TS				LP			
Ms. P		CI	AF	LP	Obs	F	R		
Mr. Y	TS	TS	F			CI			
Ms. B	CI		Me					Me	

Level 1	Level 2	Level 3
Analyzing formative data = AF	Lesson planning = LP	Providing feedback = F
Resources = R	Coteaching = CT	Demonstration lesson = D
Checking in = CI	Observing/collecting data = Obs	Teachers sharing = TS
	Meeting with team = Me	

121

and unplanned. During the brief talk, Ms. A identified two formative assessments (formal running records and answers to multiple-choice questions) that she used primarily to determine progress. The teacher and coach agreed to meet at a later date to analyze these assessments.

As they began to dig deeper into the data, other questions arose: Did the students understand the process of going back into the text to find information? What skills would they need to locate information? As the teacher and coach made a list of questions, they determined their next step: The coach would observe students and talk with them about what strategies they were using to answer the questions. The teacher was also interested in seeing if students applied different strategies based on the different types of questions they encountered. So the coach would separate her data based on questions that asked for inferential thinking and questions where the answer was literal and located in the text.

The next day, the coach pulled members of this group to talk with them about how they found the answer to questions. She wrote down her notes and shared them with the teacher. After looking through the observations, the teacher noted a trend with this group of students: They did not want to go back into the story. This group of students relied on what they remembered about the reading or what they knew about the topic based on prior knowledge. Perhaps the students needed to be explicitly taught how to go back into the text and locate information. After discussing instructional strategies, the coach and teacher determined that an explicit think-aloud process would be helpful to the students. Although the teacher had done think-alouds before where she explained her thinking process to students, she was not sure how she could demonstrate this particular skill. The coach offered to demonstrate think-alouds for the teacher and then coteach the rest of the lesson when students had opportunity to share their own think-alouds with a partner.

In terms of the gradual release of responsibility, the coach kept in mind not only that she was demonstrating think-alouds but also the process of using formative data to inform instruction. For the next phase of planning, the coach would want to check in with the teacher about student progress (again demonstrating the importance of using formative data to determine this) and also about the think-alouds. Depending on the teacher's feedback, the coach would determine her next steps for supporting the teacher by continuing to coteach to help the teacher move to the next stage of the model.

At the same time the coach is working with Ms. A, she is responsible for supporting many other teachers. Keeping track of her interactions with teachers and giving herself time to reflect on what type of support she is providing is of utmost importance in helping teachers acquire the skills and confidence they need to best help the learners in their classrooms.

The Toughest Job: Providing Meaningful Feedback

In the majority of schools, the coach might be the most knowledgeable nonclassroom teacher with regard to literacy, which makes the coach's feedback and insight very desirable and often sought after by the administration. For this reason and others, we bring up the very important distinction between providing feedback versus making evaluative comments. It is certainly the role of the coach to help the teacher reflect on his or her instruction and make judgments as to its effectiveness. However, coaches are not evaluators of instruction. Some principals may desire the coach's input when making evaluations, but we feel that you must set a clear boundary. Therefore, it is important that you and your principal clarify what your specific role will include when you work with teachers. Talk with your principal (and teachers) about the purpose of feedback from the coach and how you will give it to teachers.

We have noticed that most teachers feel uncomfortable with a coach sitting in their room for a few minutes and then leaving without having any follow-up. Sometimes, we might just share a question or observation we had about a student or tell them about our purpose for visiting their room. We never make evaluative comments such as "That was great" or "Did you know Raymond wasn't listening to your lesson" during these informal follow-ups. We also use something we call coaching clips—a quick way to communicate ideas with teachers after an informal observation. These clips, inspired by Walpole and McKenna (2004) in their book *The Literacy Coach's Handbook,* are a way we can let teachers know that our visits are not evaluative and merely a way to get more insight into teaching and learning throughout the school. We give out these clips with the hope that this will be an invitation to discuss curriculum and instruction (see Figure 31 for a sample, and see Appendix A for a

Figure 31. Sample Coaching Clips

1. Observations

> · Expectations posted and reviewed for behaviors during a teacher read-aloud
> · Focus on comprehension strategy work
> · Supportive charts around strategies
> · Teacher eliciting prior knowledge—making connection between yesterday's lesson
> · Student participation; raising hands and responding to teacher's questions

2. Considerations

> Have you considered the use of a think-pair-share as a way to provide students with a time to "rehearse" and engage with the question? This can be a way of getting more students to participate. Let me know if you want to talk more about this.

3. Celebrations

> · Teacher questions provoked deep-level thinking about books. (Students had a variety of responses about how the character changed throughout the story. Teacher encouraged them to use textual evidence to back up their ideas.)
> · Anchor charts were helpful to students, and students knew how to use them. (A number of times, students referred to the chart on how to determine the main idea.)

reproducible Coaching Clip form). Although these clips have an area for questions and celebrations, we approach these sections with the idea that whatever we might write should only open a door for coaching and not shut it by making people feel judged or evaluated.

Formal Feedback

While some teachers crave feedback—positive or negative—others fear judgment and will shy away from the process. In providing feedback to students or teachers, there are certain guidelines we have used to support a meaningful and respectful dialogue, as follows:

- Think through what feedback you want to give before the meeting.
- Schedule adequate time.
- Ask for reflection on the lesson or activity.
- Listen actively.
- Restate what is being said; ask questions to clarify any misunderstandings.
- Bring in data you have collected and analyze it together.
- Choose a limited amount of material to discuss.
- Ask participant to reflect on something positive from the lesson.
- Use data to support your ideas.
- Focus on developing solutions together.

Although some of these questions will be created as you sit and look over the data with the teacher, you may also come prepared with several questions. These questions should be nonjudgmental, should inspire teachers to think about their teaching and what students are learning, and should be tied to the data that you have collected.

Some questions to promote reflection on the data are as follows (see Appendix A for a reproducible version of these question sets):

- Let me share the data I took while I was in your class. What questions do you have after seeing this?
- Can you choose a sample where you think a student really understood _____? Why was this student successful?

- Let's look at the work of the student. What do you see here that is a strength? How can we build on this?
- What measurable goals and outcomes can we set for this student? How can I help you monitor their progress and support them?
- What do you think the data shows about _____? How can you use it in your planning?
- What does this formative assessment ask students to do? What are the subskills they need to have?
- How should we look at this data?
- What would you expect this work to look like for a __-grade student? Why do you say this?
- What criteria do you use when you look at _____?
- How do you take into account this group of learners in your planning?

Questions to promote reflection on teaching are as follows:

- I noticed that you did ____ in the lesson. Can you tell me about that?
- Talk to me about your lesson. What were the objectives and goals of the lesson? How was this articulated to students?
- What do you think students learned after the lesson? How do you know?
- Can you tell me about some of your students' learning needs? How do you know this?
- What are some ways you differentiated your teaching?
- What were you thinking while you did _____?

When teachers are feeling frustrated, you may want to offer them some of the following words of encouragement:

- So there seems to be two key issues you are discussing....
- So I hear several themes emerging....
- Considering _____, what are some tangible things I can help you with _____.
- What type of support can I provide you to help you with ___?

- I understand your frustration and know that you are doing the best you can to meet the needs of the students. Can you talk to me about areas where you see progress despite the difficulties you have faced?
- What I hear you saying is....
- What do you think would happen if....

Effective Feedback Takes Relationships Into Account

The way feedback is given must take into account the relationship that you have with the teacher. Just as an effective teacher would consider the student they are teaching and the development of the relationship, an effective coach must do the same with teachers. Try to put yourself in the shoes of the teacher with whom you are working. How many "specialists," "coaches" or instructional leaders has he or she seen in his or her career? What was the teacher's experience with them like? Does the teacher fear for his or her job? Is coaching valued at your school? Does the principal create a community where teachers are not afraid to make mistakes? It becomes very important to make a conscious effort of your demeanor, language, and nonverbal cues when talking with teachers.

Teachers that you have a more established and open relationship with may solicit your ideas by stopping you in the hallway and asking for your opinion. In these cases, you might share a thought or idea with them. However, be careful about the casual feedback scenario because often you will not have time to think carefully about what you would like to say and how you would like to say it. It is tempting, in these scenarios, to give the impromptu response that that was "a great lesson." Although time is always scarce, we have found it more effective to set up a quick meeting to provide more thoughtful feedback. We always keep in the back of our minds that it is not the job of the coach to evaluate a teacher's performance. That should be left up to the principal.

Working with adult learners requires a coach to develop various ways of providing feedback to help teachers reflect critically on their teaching. Mostly, you will see that by sharing data and carefully choosing your questions, you can assist teachers in coming to their own discoveries about teaching. No matter which category a person fits into, feedback has been used most effectively in our experience when based on data from evidence of student learning. However, the way you structure your

Table 18. Comparing Effective Feedback With Ineffective Feedback

Effective feedback	Ineffective feedback
1. Grounding feedback in student work and a preestablished focus	1. Telling teachers that you thought their lesson was "good" or "bad" or making unsolicited suggestions about what they should change
2. Asking teachers how they felt about their lesson; linking responses to evidence of student learning	2. Assuming the teacher wants feedback without first determining a focus area or context; proceeding to meet with teacher on their prep without first scheduling or agreeing on a time
3. Discussing how teachers feel most comfortable receiving feedback (meeting after school, on the phone, e-mail, etc.) and deciding on the context by which feedback is given	3. Giving the teacher feedback that is based on "what the principal wants to see"
4. Following up with teachers and checking for understanding based on the outcomes from conversations	4. Not following up with teachers or following through on previous commitments or conversations

coaching sessions and the language you use will vary depending on your relationship with the teacher and his or her experience. Some guidelines for effective feedback, compared with examples of ineffective feedback, are provided in Table 18.

As you begin to reflect on these categories, consider which one you fit into when you are given feedback about your teaching or coaching. Do you tend to be cynical, or are you open to the ideas and perspective of other educators? What is most likely to make you think deeply about your pedagogy? Thinking about yourself as a learner will help you when planning a coaching sessions with teachers.

Once the relationship with the teacher has been established, the coach can move to a more intensive stance and provide meaningful feedback and reflective dialogue to support teachers and improve student learning.

Effective Feedback Is Focused

Research on feedback shows that learning outcomes are more likely positive when feedback is task specific, rather than focused on praise or making normative comparisons (Kluger & DeNisi, 1996). Therefore, deciding what to respond to and how becomes one of your most important tasks. In many instances, you may see multiple topics requiring feedback, but you must be highly selective about what you choose to discuss with the teacher. Providing effective feedback involves choosing some talking points while ignoring others. Imagine if you were meeting with a student about a rough draft of an essay, and you had decided to focus on the content of the writing. If you responded to every spelling or grammar error in the essay, you might never get to the "meat" of the writing, or the student might become so overwhelmed that they might not be able to process your feedback. Similarly, when meeting with a teacher about the content of their writing workshop, you may have to ignore certain parts of the lesson so that you can focus on what matters more.

Effective Feedback Means Looking Ahead

Another characteristic of effective feedback is that, when possible, feedback is given before errors are made. If you are meeting with a teacher prior to the lesson and you discover that the teacher has a basic misunderstanding, you can provide proactive feedback to prevent that misunderstanding from occurring. Sometimes, you may choose to let a teacher discover a "mistake" by themselves because you feel it will be a meaningful learning situation. Other times, you will want to be proactive and prevent it before it happens.

Effective Feedback Is Continual

In the best of all possible worlds, the literacy coach would be able to visit every teacher's classroom and engage in reflective conversations on a reoccurring basis. Yet if you are like most literacy coaches, you probably do not have the time to see all teachers. It is important that each teacher you are responsible for working with gets some type of feedback from you during the year. Leaving a person out of this loop might make them feel that their exclusion is intentional or that they are doing something wrong. Often, there is a tendency to neglect the best teachers out of a confidence that they must be doing a good job. But strong teachers deserve your time as well. More often than not, they will be craving the type of reflective teaching your coaching will provide and can serve as mentors for other teachers.

Developing a workable schedule for collaborating with teachers can perhaps be the most challenging part of coaching. Some ways you can plan for developing a cycle of effective feedback with teachers are as follows:

1. List all the teachers you work with.
2. Brainstorm ways of providing feedback (e-mail, quick phone call, note, informal meeting, formal meeting).
3. Survey teachers on feedback preference.
4. Practice providing feedback with a coach/teacher and ask for their ideas about how to improve your coaching.

Depending on the nature of the school, your other responsibilities as literacy coach—and the number of teachers you work with—you will probably struggle to develop ways to provide teachers with meaningful feedback. How can you manage to see everyone and provide support for them in addition to all your other duties? Through our experience, we have found that not every teacher will need the same type or amount of support. As you develop relationships with teachers and understand the needs of their students, time can be used much more efficiently and effectively.

Feedback Is a Two-Way Street

When people think about feedback in the coaching situation, many still fall back on the model where the coach provides feedback about a lesson or part of instruction. However, it is important to consider when the teacher has a chance to share feedback about your coaching. The Coaching Clip (see Figure 31 on page 124) may inspire teachers to give feedback or share their thoughts, but there are other opportunities coaches might provide to enable teachers' feedback. Perhaps they may need something from you that could help them in their teaching, if you simply knew about it. Some teachers prefer getting feedback in written form so they have time to think about it, while others want it face to face. Asking teachers for their input about your coaching will once again show your willingness to put yourself on the line, just like you are asking them to do.

Formative Coaching Case Study

We have provided the following case study to show how a coach might use the information from Chapters 3 and 4 to support teachers as they make meaning from student work and develop targeted plans of action. In this scenario, we see an example of how a coach introduces the formative cycle to a grade-level team that wants to learn more about students' reading fluency, selects a protocol to analyze this data with the team, and then tracks the type of support she offers to the individual teachers.

Scenario: They Read Too Slowly!

Grade level: Three second-grade teachers

Experience looking at student work as a formative assessment: Varied

Relationship between coach and teachers: Have cotaught with two of the teachers

Expected reaction to looking at student work: Positive

Focus: Looking at fluency passages

The Scenario. After looking at the fluency rates from a DIBELS assessment, the second-grade team is concerned by the number of students who were just under the cutoff for the benchmark fluency assessment. Reading fluency refers to the ability of readers to read quickly, effortlessly, and efficiently with good, meaningful expression (Rasinski, 2003). Reading fluency has, for years, been called a missing ingredient in many reading programs (Allington, 1993). Initially, the focus is on words per minute. Although they haven't missed the benchmark by many words, many students are still below the expected number of words per minute.

Preparing. Although you have met with this team before, brought them resources, even cotaught with two of the teachers, you have never used the formative coaching cycle with this team. You have also provided support for this grade level, but you worry that it has never been consistent. You decide that you would like to integrate the formative coaching cycle with this team.

Meeting. When you start your meeting, you can tell the team is distraught, specifically by the number of students who they felt were doing quite well who are not meeting the number of words per minute to be deemed on grade level according to DIBELS. The team seems disheartened by their data, as though they themselves have received a failing grade. You decide to introduce them to the idea of formative analysis by demonstrating how they might use this fluency data (see Figure 4 on page 17 in Chapter 1) to help plan future instruction. You decide to look at one of the teacher's just-below benchmark data as an example (see Table 19).

Because the teachers have just done a fluency read with the students, you explain to them that you are actually beginning at the fourth step of the cycle—digging into the data. The team seems relieved not to have to go through the first three steps. The criteria for "fluent reading" is already predetermined by the DIBELS assessment, as were the three categories of students: intensive, strategic, and benchmark. While only the benchmark students were deemed on target for their grade level, the strategic and intensive groups were considered at risk because their fluency scores were not meeting the fluency rate for second grade. In essence, the quick sort has already been done for the grade.

The teachers start by focusing their attention on the strategic group. While looking at the scores is a good starting point, the team soon realizes it is not giving them the answers that they need. They decide to turn to the actual assessments. As they look through the fluency reads for this middle group, they see that there are some words that the majority of students stumbled on or missed when reading.

Table 19. Teacher's DIBELS Data

Strategic group	Words per minute (target rate = 68 wpm)
Jimmy P.	48
Raymond H.	59
Alisa W.	61
Robyn A.	55
Michelle M.	45
Lila B.	64

You decide to begin the conversation with the trendspotting technique (see Chapter 3). You use this as a way to warm up and help teachers become more comfortable with making observations based on data from the student work. As Mr. V looks through the work, he notices a trend: Words such as *decided, parents,* and *family* were causing students difficulty. He says that these words are so common in second-grade books that one would hope that students do not need to sound them out; these words are high-frequency words and should be read with automaticity. As you begin to think about lessons, you ask the teachers about their sight word lists. The team has a grade-level sight word list of about 50 words, but as they reflect on these words, they seem to be very basic and more appropriate for a first-grade class. The teachers then begin to look at their notes about how this middle group fared on a sight word assessment. It seems that the students were able to automatically name these 50 words without mistakes.

Another observation made by one of the teachers is that when students from the strategic group read, they did not notice phrases. Instead, she explains, they read word by word. "This could have slowed them down," points out Ms. G. "Maybe helping students to recognize phrases in their reading would be helpful."

After talking informally for awhile, the group decides to use the BEST Assignment Analysis Protocol (see Chapter 3 and Appendix B) to continue their discussion and help investigate the underlying skills to reading fluently (see Figure 32). Because they have already had some discussion, the group moves quickly through each section, using the graphic organizer to jot down their insights. When they get to the section of the protocol that begins to talk about feedback, they decide that they have not spent much time thinking about how to share results with students and parents. The team decides to provide weekly feedback to students about their fluency by giving each student a fluency graph. As a group, you brainstorm future ideas, and then the teachers choose which ones they would like to try out. They choose to (1) discuss with students the purpose of reading fluently, (2) practice automaticity of reading higher-level sight words, (3) focus on repeated reading during shared reading and independent reading time, and (4) incorporate the teaching of simple phrases. They decided that the first three ideas would be appropriate for

Figure 32. Analysis of Assignments Used for Increasing Reading Fluency

Assignment type	
Goal of assignment	Fluent reading of grade-level text
Break it down • Subskills contained within assignment • Important vocabulary/concepts to teach	· Student understands purpose of reading fluently (they should know that they can't spend too long on one word) · Knowledge and automaticity of sight words · Ability to read phrases · Recognition of punctuation · Strategies to solve unknown words
Exemplars • What kind of models/examples can I provide for students to know what good work looks like?	· Fluency practice with class poems · Fluency practice with Readers Theatre (teacher monitored) · Partner practice · Listening to stories on tape · Repeated readings
Schedule it • When will I teach these skills (subskills)? • When will I provide feedback?	· Practice shared reading passages/poems (daily) · Find sight words in reading (daily at reading center) · Strategic group practice of phrases (daily during center time) · Small-group reading time with teacher/Readers Theatre · Phrase boards throughout the school (on the way to lunch or the bathroom) · Repeated readings of leveled independent reading books (daily for 10 minutes)
Track it • How will I monitor my students' progress? • How will I provide feedback about this?	· Fluency monitoring—Students will read weekly to teacher and have an individual graph noting their rates

all the learners in their class, while explicit teaching of phrases might be best for students from the benchmark and strategic.

As the team discusses their ideas, they also determine further formative assessments that they want to do with students to understand more about students' reading. They decide that they will do running records for the group of children in the middle group because they want more information about these students. The team decides they will then analyze these running records to understand students' reading and comprehension. They will include descriptive notes about students' fluency, noting whether students use punctuation and read word by word or in phrases.

Follow-Up. Over the next two weeks, you record the different types of support that you give the teachers (see Figure 30 on page 121; a reproducible form that can help you track your coaching activities can be found in Appendix A). Out of the three teachers, one requests your support in their classroom in using Readers Theatre to help build students' literacy skills. You meet with Mr. V during his free period and go over some ideas on how to use Readers Theatre to support fluency in the classroom. You both decide that you will introduce it to the small group over a few days while Mr. V watches and listens as students independently practice the script. Mr. V is curious to see who will be on task and also what resources they will use when they come to a word they do not know. Together, you and Mr. V develop a chart to note this student behavior so that you can later discuss it (see Figure 33). This will help you begin the cycle again.

The support you continue to provide the teachers ranges from informal check-ins to locating resources about fluency or collaborating with the teacher in their classroom. As you work more with the students

Figure 33. Form Created By Teacher and Coach to Measure Fluency

Student	Asks a friend	Skips word	Uses a chart	Sounds it out
Layla		✓		
Joseph			✓	
Kevin			✓	✓

in these classes, new questions arise in your mind that pertain more to whole-school issues. What do we do in kindergarten and first grade to help students' fluency? What happens when students leave second grade and they are not judged as fluent according to these standards? How many of our third graders are struggling with comprehension due to fluency? As you think about these questions, you begin to ponder how important it is to work in a school where teachers from various grade levels collaborate with one another to improve student achievement. How can you go about creating a community of committed professionals who work together? Chapter 5 will address many of these questions.

REFLECTING AND EXTENDING

Formative information can take many different forms. Classroom observations are another great data source that you can use while going through the formative analysis cycle. In this chapter, we covered a number of different observational tools that can help bring focus and make meaning of the goings-on of a classroom. As you analyze formative information with teachers, you will find yourself collaborating in classrooms, providing demonstration lessons, or even coteaching or planning a lesson. Preparing for collaboration is always important, as is following up your session with feedback that promotes reflection about teaching and learning. While providing feedback can be one of the most challenging tasks of a coach, the formative coaching cycle supports the coach in consistently engaging teachers in thinking about the needs of learners and the various types of instructional choices that will be effective for students.

QUESTIONS TO CONSIDER

1. Describe a lesson that you demonstrated for a teacher. How did the lesson come about? What was the outcome of modeling the lesson?

2. Consider the Coaching Activities and Levels of Intensity Chart (see Table 14 on page 94). Which level do your coaching activities fit into?

3. How do you feel about providing feedback to a teacher about his or her instruction? What are some phrases you have used that help promote reflection?

4. What are some focused observations that you have done or want to try? Why do you think this information can be useful?

CHAPTER 5

The Huddle: Developing the Professional Learning Community

Imagine This!

Things are going well with your individual coaching and conference sessions. You've been meeting with teachers regularly, modeling for others, and team teaching with a few. As a result you are starting to notice trends across grade levels. After looking through a recent schoolwide assessment, it is apparent that students are struggling with vocabulary questions that ask them to locate the meaning of unknown words in reading passages. You discuss this with some teachers, and they confirm what you are thinking—the students are taught every year how to find the meaning of a word through the context of the sentence but they rarely use this strategy independently nor do they make it a point to transfer use of new vocabulary in their writing, reading, or speech. It seems to be a concern that is voiced throughout your school.

You know that teachers would benefit by meeting together to look at student work collaboratively to help students extend their vocabulary and identify strategies that the whole school can use. But when exactly will this meeting take place? You have so few professional development days as it is, and the district prescribes most of the topics. Would teachers be willing to meet on their own time or during grade-level preps? Will they want to share their work or will they see this as intrusive? And most importantly, will they value the ideas of their colleagues? How can you help teachers look beyond their own grade level and begin to see the important role of each classroom in making all students literate?

The term *professional learning community* has become a buzzword in the current world of education. DuFour and Eaker (1998) describe a professional learning community as a community composed of collaborative teams whose members work interdependently to achieve common goals linked to the purpose of learning for all.

Think about working in a school that has no professional learning community. Doors are shut tightly. At 2:30 the bell rings, and the students go home. The teachers continue to grade papers in their room or follow the students out each day. There is no dialogue about teaching in the hallways, at staff meetings, or during grade-level preps. As a result, things continue as they always have—business as usual. Taken on the surface, the definition of a professional learning community may sound simple and be interpreted by some as teachers meeting together, discussing a topic, and then completing an evaluation form at the end of the meeting. However, a true professional learning community is not just one that is intended to discuss frustrations, complaints, and observations about their classroom or school. The very essence of a professional learning community is a focus on a commitment to the learning of each student (DuFour, DuFour, Eaker, & Many, 2006).

Depending on your school and principal, you may already work in a setting with a thriving professional learning community, one that values collaboration, has time for teacher input, and is ripe for a focus on analyzing student work to improve academic achievement and instruction. Building a professional learning community can be a daunting and difficult task. In some ways, as a coach, it would be easier to just meet with teachers individually to discuss new strategies and implement various techniques, but a collective responsibility is necessary to build a trusting community that will look at student work collectively and make the necessary changes to improve teaching and learning. Choosing to develop and grow a professional learning community will not only help a school to meet the needs of the students but also develop and expand the capacity of the staff.

However, the road to building a professional learning community may initially be paved with more questions than answers. Who will initiate the process? What will be the organizing principle behind the community? Will everyone be involved from the start or is there a leadership team that will spearhead the work? If separate committees and communities already exist in the school, how will the community come together on one accord?

As literacy coaches, when we first began to think about the idea of a professional learning community, we started by reading about professional learning communities and reflecting on the community at our own school. Time was set aside during one of the professional development school days to get feedback from teachers by reading about professional learning communities, examining case studies, and discussing the type of community we envisioned as a school. We established group norms and created a group symbol of an elephant, derived from a National Geographic video of a herd of elephants helping out a smaller elephant who had become stuck in a ditch. The visual we showed the staff was to serve as a reminder to work together to achieve a common goal and to think back to the norms and values of our professional learning community when times got rough; the only way we'd be able to move through the difficult times would be to work collaboratively. The group norms we established are as follows:

- Be respectful.
- Allow space and time for reflection.
- Listen to one another.
- Actively participate.
- Keep an open mind.

Next, along with the help of our leadership team and administration, we developed four clear steps to help us get the ball rolling for our professional learning community:

1. Research and define the meaning of a professional learning community.
2. Determine how to approach human resources and structural resources within your professional learning community.
3. Target three literacy priorities of the professional learning community.
4. Assess and celebrate community progress.

These steps can be used at any school to help to initiate, build, and strengthen the professional learning community around literacy teaching and learning.

Step 1: Research and Define the Meaning of a Professional Learning Community

Although it may seem obvious at first, the initial step to building a professional learning community is to make sure that the staff is aware of the commitment to developing it. Some teachers may not be familiar with this term or there may be various interpretations of the term throughout the building. For example, in the earlier definition by DuFour and Eaker (1998), how will you define what "learning for all" means? Is it test scores? High school acceptance letters? Are teachers and administrators included in the "all" of the above definition? Most teachers would agree that the purpose of education is to provide learning for all students; however, the method by which we pursue this purpose is often ambiguous or fragmented at best. While the coming together to discuss ideas and research is often the first step in establishing a professional learning community, the community itself is not devoid of accountability or responsibility. These communities consist of teachers and administrators who continuously seek and share learning and then act on what they learn (Astuto, Clark, Read, McGree, & Fernandez, 1993). Once schools define the meaning of a professional learning community and decide to collectively commit to building and growing their community, they can set goals or establish priorities within their community. The goals of the community should also be based on formative data (feedback from teachers, needs assessments, focus groups, and student data and feedback) and include a strong focus on looking at student work to improve instruction and student achievement.

Facilitating the evolution and development of the community occurs over a sustained period of time. To establish a common philosophy of teaching and learning that is not only espoused but practiced, teachers must be afforded multiple opportunities within a structured environment to share new ideas, grow as individual professionals, and reflect on academic progress. At first it may seem awkward, even unnatural, to sit together as a school or cluster team to discuss student work and instructional strategies. However the coming together as a community must be developed until it is natural, spontaneous, and a logical next step based on the thoughtful instruction that teachers are demonstrating in their classroom. Collaboration enables teachers to test their ideas about teaching and expand their level of expertise by allowing them to hear the ideas of others (Wildman & Niles, 1987). The community itself should provide a safe haven where ideas can be challenged, fears can be verbalized, and creativity explored. In addition to engaging in reflective dialogue, teachers must also have a support system and ongoing professional development to enable them to apply and refine what they've learned.

Throughout recent years, the research about professional learning communities has become more comprehensive and accessible to schools. It is important to arm yourself as well as your school with research to validate your concerns and to realize that much of what you will experience is also the experience of other professionals in leadership roles who are attempting to build a professional learning community.

Here are some questions to ponder as you begin thinking about how you will define, establish, or grow the professional learning community at your school:

- How does the school define or discuss the meaning and definition of a professional learning community?
- What is the understanding of the leadership team or administration about professional learning communities?
- How does the staff currently view the professional learning community?
- What is the principal's background or knowledge about professional learning communities?
- How does the community engage, share, and celebrate progress with parents and other stakeholders?
- What leverage (i.e. established grade-level teams, time for professional development, an understanding of how professional learning communities develop and evolve, etc.) already exists within the professional learning community to access for development?

Step 2: Determine How to Approach Human Resources and Structural Resources Within Your Professional Learning Community

Extensive research from Kruse, Louis, and Bryk (1994) shows that certain conditions must be met in order for a professional learning community to develop and grow within a school. They have broken these conditions into two categories: human—or social—resources and structural resources. Human resources deal with social issues, such as trust, communication, and an intrinsic commitment to improvement and supportive leadership. Structural resources deal with issues around things we call the infrastructure of the school. This includes time to meet, the organization of meetings, and systems that must be put in place to ensure that the work and goals of the community can physically and realistically be pursued. It is necessary for schools to address and balance both conditions respectively to establish a thriving professional learning community.

Human Resources

At our school—although we were armed with research, knowledge, and experience—deciding to consciously build a professional learning community and focus on the human resources aspect was no easy task. How do you take a group of individuals with their own set of concerns and their own understanding about how schools and classrooms should function and build a cohesive group that works to help students achieve? Many teachers who smiled amicably at one another in the hall did not necessarily know one another or want to work together. Yet we knew the work we needed to do as a school would involve a high level of commitment, collaboration, and trust from the adults in the building. Our school was not a blank slate upon which we could impose our views of what a professional community would be like. The teachers already worked in an environment that had its own professional climate. They had history, experience with one another, relationships with students, and a variety of preconceived notions or beliefs that made forming a professional learning community more or less likely, depending on the circumstance.

Established were the many roles teachers played within our community. There were the "knowledgeable teachers," the "newbies," the "complainers," the "comedians," the "collaborators," and the "individuals," all of which were shaping our community. There were informal rules established: who talked during our whole-school professional development meetings, who would stand up and be the voice of reason, who would remain silent, and who would go on grading their papers. But as we continued to build relationships with the staff and learned how to take the information we observed and interpret it in a meaningful way, we realized that each person had something valuable they could bring to the team and, at the very least, provided a learning experience from which we would grow as coaches. For example, the staff member who may have been seen as "questioning authority" or the "dissenter" was actually the person who helped us question our own methods of coaching and leadership. The person who may have sat in meetings grading papers or engaging in small talk made us think about the purpose of our professional development for the day. Did this session apply directly to them? Was it thoughtfully crafted and differentiated as we had come to expect in lessons for our students? As coaches and instructional leaders, being part of a community meant we played a role, which carried a responsibility as well. We constantly reexamined our own contributions, reflected on the example we were setting, and modeled the characteristics we wanted to see demonstrated in the community.

Think about the individuals in your community, and consider the following questions to begin assessing your human and social resources:

- Are individuals willing to meeting regularly as a school or as a cluster about literacy?
- Are teachers willing to collaborate and meet together outside of school hours?
- Does the culture support teachers expressing differing opinions or ideas about literacy instruction?
- Is there a basic level of trust and respect in the school community?
- Are teachers willing to seek out help in areas of need and not fear being punished for doing so?
- Do teachers trust you in your role as a literacy coach? Do you continually make efforts to build and sustain their trust?
- Does the principal support the idea of a professional learning community and promote collaboration and professional dialogue?
- Do teachers discuss lesson plans, ideas for activities, or share resources on their own?

As our school reflected on these questions and assessed our own community, a group of traits emerged that enabled us to articulate a common vision of what our professional learning community should look like (see Table 20). These characteristics were not actualized after one or two meetings or conversations but after years of collaborative research about professional learning communities, a courageous effort to be reflective as a school, and a commitment to seeking better versions of ourselves as educators. As we continued to build and grow, these traits became evident and could be seen, heard, and felt throughout the building.

While your school may not currently display the characteristics of a thriving professional learning community, we are confident each school has the seeds and fertile ground necessary to establish itself on a continuum of a high-functioning professional learning community. In fact, the more tumultuous or unsettling a community, the more ripe it may be for the work that is necessary for building a professional learning community. Oftentimes the struggles, frustrations, and trials in a school

Table 20. Characteristics of a Thriving Professional Learning Community

What it looks like
- Time for collaboration and reflective dialogue
- Emphasis on examining formative data and the work of the students
- Willingness to make teachers' practice public, talk about their teaching, and share planning ideas
- Openness to collaborating and accepting feedback
- Willingness to implement new ideas and reflect on their effectiveness
- Common goals that can be articulated throughout the building

What it sounds like
- Conversations that demonstrate a sense of efficacy among teachers
- Questioning of your own practice
- Inquiry among staff
- Shared language in describing instruction and assessment
- Celebration and encouragement of feedback

What it feels like
- Accountability focused on supporting student learning rather than assigning blame
- Ongoing support by colleagues
- Trust between staff members and administration
- Safe haven for critical thinking and questioning
- Support for new and veteran teachers
- Community norms that are established and respected
- Common goal or vision toward which everyone is moving

shore up the demand for some type of organizational structure and norms that an active professional learning community will provide. A coach's role might be to provide support in tiny, incremental nudges to get the ball rolling. The coach may also play a big part in organizing and developing the structural resources to support the professional learning community.

Structural Resources

While each school can be placed at different points on a continuum of a working professional learning community, every school already has a community in the basic sense of the word: a culture and a climate that is prevalent throughout the building. In some cases, school communities are formed by default. However, to produce lasting and authentic results to improve student achievement, the community must be formed by design. Having the time, space, clear outcomes, and established goals for regular grade-level meetings and cluster or cycle meetings are all examples of communities formed by design.

If there is not a regular time, procedure, or protocol for meeting, then the community will not have the outlet or opportunity to collaborate and grow. Within every thriving community, there are regular meetings, forums for discussions, methods for gaining feedback, identified roles and responsibilities, and opportunities for growth and contribution. The infrastructure or structural resources provide the mechanism for all of this to happen. With an established infrastructure and the identification and development of a school's structural resources, long-term professional development and routines can be established (see Figure 34 for example of a grade-level project planning guide, and see Appendix A for a reproducible version of this guide).

As your school thinks of ideas, techniques, and strategies for working toward a thriving professional community, many factors will have to be taken into consideration, such as the following:

- Are there clear roles in the professional learning community? How are they defined, and how do the people in these roles support the structural resources?
- Is the principal committed to providing opportunities for teachers to collaborate?

Figure 34. Sample Grade-Level Project Planning Guide

Purpose of the project

1. To strengthen pillars (Kruse, Louis, & Bryk, 1994) of our professional learning community, we need
   - Deprivitization of practice
   - Collaborative workplace
   - Reflective dialogue
   - Shared values and norms
   - Student-centered focus

2. To develop a deeper understanding of the following reading strategies: questioning, determining importance, synthesizing, inferring, making connections, visualizing

3. To develop an understanding of how the specific strategies support student comprehension

4. To examine and identify instructional strategies and activities that support strategies

5. To examine student work and formative assessments produced from activities aligned with the strategies

6. To begin forming vertical alignment and scaffolding of reading strategies to support schoolwide comprehension

Outcomes

1. Have a better understanding of how to utilize the reading strategies to build student comprehension

2. Learned new activities and instructional approaches to teaching strategies

3. Reflected on a lesson or activity based on one of the reading strategies

4. Examined student work produced from activities focusing on the strategies

5. Integrated all strategies into curriculum maps for 08-09

6. Read from <u>Strategies That Work</u> to strengthen understanding

7. Shared findings and information with staff during 20-minute presentation

- Does the principal value teacher autonomy and view teachers as professionals?
- Is there regular time for teachers to meet that is embedded within the school day or immediately after school?
- Are meetings held frequently enough so that teachers can connect and have meaningful conversations?
- Is there a designated leader facilitating the grade level or cluster meetings? Is there an agenda with a clear purpose and specific outcomes?
- Is there a grade-level or cycle representative to act as a point person to disseminate and share information?
- Is there an accountability measure in place for the information presented and shared at the meeting?
- Are there opportunities for shared leadership and celebration?
- How will progress throughout the school be shared and celebrated?
- Are there multiple means of communication within the infrastructure, such as e-mail and newsletters?

The Balancing Act

Addressing the basic issues and needs within the structural and human resource conditions will allow schools to more effectively move toward a thriving professional learning community. Most schools will not solely focus on literacy within their professional learning communities, but for many schools literacy may act as a springboard or model for how the community will operate in other areas. Within the context of the community, it is important to emphasize that the focus on human and structural resources must be balanced.

For example, one of the initial challenges some communities might face is finding time to actually get together to discuss issues that affect student learning. Although we agree that creating a time and space for reflective thinking and collaboration is essential, often the human resources are more critical to the development of the professional community than structural resources are (Kruse et al., 1994). No matter how much time is allocated for community collaboration or how the professional development calendar is structured, there may never be enough time to satisfy everyone. Another factor to consider is the stamina or mental energy of teachers when considering issues of time. It is not enough for a school's leadership to simply tack another period onto the end of the workday that is already long and tiring; such periods must be built into the school's schedule and calendar in a way that gives teachers opportunities to consider critical issues in a reflective manner (Kruse et al., 1994). Striking a balance takes finesse and careful planning among the leadership team; too much time without clear goals, outcomes, or purpose will squander resources and not necessarily result in student achievement or build teacher capacity. On the other hand, having a staff with great ideas, excellent communication, and a commitment to examine evidence of student learning without the provision of time allocated by the administration may lead to frustration and burnout and may send the message that the administration does not support or respect the work of the teachers. When schools can address both of these conditions in a thoughtful and consistent manner, schools can work more efficiently to address the work of the community.

Step 3: Target Three Literacy Priorities for the Professional Learning Community

After reviewing the first two steps, your school may engage in research about the professional learning community and agree on a common definition and characteristics for the community. In addition, the administration and leadership team may have created a plan to address the structural and human conditions within the school community. So, now what?

In our school, as we met more frequently and purposefully to develop our community, it became apparent very quickly in our discussions that we did not all share the same literacy vision, goals, and outcomes for our students. Sure we had our state-developed language arts standards and school-created curriculum maps. But as we looked at the formative data and student work, questions, confusion, and echoes of concern were expressed, such as the following examples:

- How was the first-grade teacher defining "at grade level" for her students? And what assessments were they using to determine this?

- What criteria were being used by the eighth-grade team to determine if a graduating student was ready for high school?
- What standard or rubric was being used to determine proficiency in writing?

And once these questions were allowed to surface, it was the foundation we established within our professional learning community that enabled us to successfully facilitate these difficult conversations, making sure discussions remained respectful, responses tactful, and all feedback leading back to supporting one another as we built our own capacity as educators. From these discussions, we collectively identified three shared priorities to continue to develop our professional learning community around literacy:

1. Establishing a shared language (common language and instructional coherence)
2. Developing shared responsibility (job-embedded professional development)
3. Cultivating shared leadership (building teacher efficacy)

Shared Language—Common Language and Instructional Coherence

Most communities already have a mission, vision, and philosophy for their school. According to Nanus (1992), there is no more powerful engine driving an organization toward excellence and long-range success than an attractive, worthwhile, and achievable vision of the future that is widely shared. However, how many schools have a vision for literacy at their school and share a common language about its practice?

Think of a classroom teacher reviewing the understanding of main idea with her class. The teacher constructed a meaning together with the class defining the main idea and applied it through various learning activities. A visitor walks in and asks what the students are doing. The student replies, "We are identifying the main idea in the text." The visitor says, "Interesting! Can you tell me what main idea means?" The teacher looks on and anxiously waits for the reply. Will the student say the definition they created together? Will the student share a definition of another strategy? Or will the student bleakly reply, "I don't know"?

Furthermore, does the "correct" response of the student really mean that the concept is being applied or used appropriately and demonstrate understanding of main idea? Much like the teacher who is waiting for the student's response, as a coach it is interesting to see how the staff would respond to a question about the mission of the school, the vision, or the goals for literacy. Will they recite a scripted answer, come up with an authentic response, or simply reply, "I don't know"?

Shared language among staff within the school is equally as important as shared language among students within the classroom. While we all might not understand every word, concept, or phrase in the English language, the fact that we are speaking the same language helps us to move in the right direction. For the vision, mission, and philosophy to become a reality, there must be a common language, a common practice, and a willingness to continually evaluate the language and practice to ensure it resonates, carrying significant meaning to the staff. A vision will have little impact until it is widely shared and accepted and until it connects with the personal visions of those within the school (DuFour & Eaker, 1998).

As the literacy coach, think about the vision for literacy at your school. How does it align with the mission and philosophy of your school? If you don't have a clear vision for literacy teaching and learning at your school, your leadership team and staff can create one together to help ground your professional learning community.

To help establish a common understanding, schools can begin the conversation by discussing the vision for the highest grade (or graduating class) at their school. This process can be done with the school as an entire community or in small clusters and then shared with the community as a whole. Here are some questions that the coach can ask to help facilitate the process:

- Do we have a current vision for literacy at our school?
- How does this vision support the graduating class?
- What is our literacy vision for our graduating class? What do we expect them to be able to do upon graduating in terms of comprehension, word knowledge, fluency, and writing?
- How will each grade level support this vision?

- If we seek to realize this vision, what would be our mission to achieve the vision?
- What philosophy would we have to embody to ground us in this vision and mission? How does this relate to our current philosophy?

Therefore, the literacy vision we created together at NTA was "NTA students will be able to utilize a variety of strategies, literary experiences, and educational opportunities to build and improve reading comprehension and written expression in order to affect change in their world and communicate effectively."

As coaches we also thought about the type of professional development we would have to provide teachers with to support our literacy vision and philosophy. An example of the philosophy for literacy at our school that came out of our vision was "NTA students will be met at their instructional level and set goals towards improvement in reading comprehension. Reading is taught through a balanced literacy approach to ensure students have a wide access to a variety of literature, genres, and instructional strategies. Teachers serve as the facilitator in the classroom and gradually release responsibility to students to empower them as readers and writers."

One of the greatest benefits of the creation of our vision and philosophy was the shift in conversations and development of instructional coherence around literacy in our building. How could we expect to achieve a common vision for the graduating eighth grader if coherence across the grades was inconsistent or unclear from one classroom to the next?

Like other successful schools, we worked diligently to ensure the vision was more than just words on paper. Our vision is constantly being revisited and revised. Whether a school is led by a principal or a site-based team, that leader must be a prime "keeper" of the school's vision (Kruse et al., 1994).

Shared Responsibility—Job-Embedded Professional Development

The term *professional development* has come to have different meanings depending on the individual experience—to some it means a half-hour to two-hour workshop, focusing on a specific topic; to others it might mean a course or class at a university; and to others the term might include engaging in an action research group with a team of teachers. These are all definitions we use to describe professional development; however, it is the job-embedded professional development specifically that made the most significant impact on academic achievement and individual professional growth.

Job-embedded professional development refers to learning that takes place during the course of one's work, where daily access to necessary materials, knowledge, and assistance are readily available (Arkansas Department of Education, 2006). More specifically, job-embedded professional development can also include conversations in the hallway about best practices, the impromptu meetings in the lounge about teaching strategies, and the e-mail exchanges that interpret assessment data. When professional development becomes job embedded, it then becomes everyone's responsibility to participate and to ensure that interactions provide meaningful results with measurable growth for the teacher and the students. Typically when professional development is given in a whole-group format, where teachers sit and receive information, the sharing of information and shared responsibility for utilizing the information can be lost or becomes secondary to other factors.

Before we shifted our focus to job-embedded professional development, our whole-group sessions often concluded with conversations among teachers about our delivery of the workshop or the questioning of its relevance to their daily practice. Once we began to work more collaboratively with teachers in the classrooms and allowed them the opportunity to coplan and even lead professional development, they became participants as opposed to spectators and took more ownership over the learning process. Job-embedded professional development is also more aligned with research about adult learners (as discussed in Chapter 1). There are key points to remember about quality job-embedded professional development:

- It needs to be relevant and applicable to the teacher.
- It should link back to the overall literacy goals for your school.
- It should be ongoing and continuous.
- It should provide a space for reflection and construction of knowledge.
- It should build teacher efficacy and support teacher autonomy.

Because formative coaching is rooted in the analysis of student work, coaches can use formative data to provide teachers with ongoing job-embedded professional development with one-on-one coaching as well as schoolwide coaching. Looking at student work collectively will enable communities to address the characteristics of quality job-embedded professional development.

For example, let's say a coach is going to facilitate a grade-level or cluster-cycle meeting, using a student work sample to provide a context for job-embedded professional development. As a result, one of the teachers agrees to bring a sample of a student's work, seeking feedback from the community about additional methods to help the student, who is struggling in reading and writing. The group uses the following protocol to discuss the student's work:

1. Teacher states the dilemma in the form of a question to the group.

2. Other group members ask clarifying questions about the problem.

3. Teacher states possible reasons why student is struggling based on other formative data and techniques that have been implemented.

4. Group members chart possible reasons shared and techniques implemented.

5. Group looks at student work sample(s).

6. Group members individually jot down strengths and weaknesses they notice (share strengths and weaknesses using the phrase "I noticed...").

7. Group members give feedback about the problem and may offer another alternative; group members build on techniques implemented or offer new direction (share recommendations using the phrase "I wonder...").

Although the members of the team may be discussing one student from a particular teacher's classroom, all of the members will contribute and therefore learn in the process. It is more than likely the participating teachers have a student with similar characteristics in their own classroom, and teachers will also have the opportunity to learn about the philosophies of one another as well as resources or materials they may have to lend support. This example illustrates the use of job-embedded support: The teachers are looking at real work from students in their classroom or building, the teachers are using their own expertise and knowledge to contribute to the growth of the professional community, the teachers are creating real solutions that they can implement, and the coach can support the teachers based on authentic data and can provide additional feedback or resources to support the student.

In addition, job-embedded professional development should encourage educators to view daily experiences as opportunities to learn (Wood & McQuarrie, 1999). The notion of job-embedded professional development, in fact, is what inspired the idea of formative coaching. Our struggling eighth graders that we all committed to supporting at our school would not have a fighting chance in reaching the vision set forth without quality and consistent professional development within a growing professional learning community. As coaches, we believe the task of planning, organizing, and evaluating professional development is a shared responsibility. This responsibility may be shared by planning lessons collaboratively, team teaching, or arranging peer observations. Teachers then have the opportunity to reflect and actually see how the information discussed in an article, at a meeting, or through a video will play out authentically in their classroom with their particular group of students. As a result, teachers will see the coach as a partner in literacy as opposed to an administrator or manager of literacy.

Another added benefit of job-embedded support is that it will allow professional development to occur during the school day, alleviating the tension of always having to do professional development after school, which further extends the school day. While all schools may not have the same amount of designated time to block out units of space for schoolwide professional development, schools can create a plan for job-embedded professional development.

The work of the literacy coach in their daily responsibilities often contains many examples of job-embedded professional development. Our goal is to support coaches in making that support more focused, meaningful, and directly linked to the evidence of student learning. Clarifying broad professional development goals also helps to determine what type of resources, research, and tools are necessary to build as steppingstones to meet our goals. The following is an example of our initial mission and goals for our professional development; these were created with the staff and revisited each year:

Professional development mission: To provide meaningful professional development that will support academic achievement and deepen understanding of best literacy practices

Goals

- Create professional learning communities that engage in reflective dialogue and meaningful conversation around student work and literacy instruction
- Develop teacher leaders to facilitate and participate in meaningful conversations around academic achievement through the analysis of formative data
- Gradually release responsibility to support teachers to independently and collectively engage in regular practice
- Analyze student work and identify needs for differentiation
- Plan activities and assessments based on needs and formative data
- Reflect on teaching and instructional strategies through journaling, dialogues, or conferences
- Independently utilize and identify research to support effective literacy teaching and learning

As the professional learning community continues to thrive and develop, schools may then create specific outcomes to measure the goals of the community.

There are certain traditions that communities engage in to build cohesion and tradition. The establishment of the rituals and routines help staff members feel as if they are a part of a community and give members a sense of predictability and familiarity that provides a level of comfort and security. This enables teachers to take risks and also provides the opportunity for the community to evolve by working to improve or creatively enhance existing rituals and routines that might need to be revisited. Rituals and routines also help new staff members to establish an understanding about the norms of operation in a building. For example, if a new staff member joined your community what routines would they be able to readily observe and support? What values would be evident? What are the unspoken traditions and routines of the community as well as the obvious traditions?

One of the most successful rituals and routines put in place to sustain our professional learning community included regular grade-level team meetings and intermittent cycle-cluster meetings. Each grade level had at least one planning period during the week that was in common. Grade levels chose a team leader that would facilitate the meetings, keep records of attendance, and ensure the agenda and outcomes of the meeting were aligned with the school's goals and vision. Each week the grade-level teams would submit a feedback form to the principal and request any additional support or clarifications for next steps. Topics for the grade-level agenda might include

- Looking at student work
- Planning lessons based on analysis
- Gathering and sharing resources
- Planning interventions or enrichment opportunities for individual or groups of students

The common grade-level planning periods also provided us with a set time when we knew all grade-level members would be together. As coaches, this enabled us to sit in on meetings to listen or request time on the agenda to share information or address specific concerns. However, we did not lead or run the meetings, as this was the responsibility of the grade-level team members. Reviewing the notes of the meeting in the event that we could not attend also provided us with valuable information about the progress of the team and additional support to provide. We encouraged grade-level team members to see this as hundreds of minutes together across a semester as opposed to 40 minutes a week. Our cluster-cycle meetings provided an extension to the grade-level meetings in order to foster communication across all grade levels in our building.

One of our greatest benefits to this ritual and routine was the involvement of special education in this process. As our entire school began to use the formative coaching cycle, much of the work we were doing through our collaborative efforts were already implemented in pockets of our school in special education classrooms. Looking closely at student work, setting goals and targets through individualized education plans, and monitoring progress at benchmarked points throughout the year were all familiar practices of our special education program. Supporting our school with methods for differentiation and helping to identify and diagnose specific reading difficulties was also another benefit to our collaborative efforts. As a result, literacy coaches need to internalize the tenet that special education teachers should be included regularly in professional development (Jay & Strong, 2008). The special education teachers and regular education teachers have much to share and much to offer in meeting the various needs of the students. Difficulty with learning to read is a primary characteristic of children placed in special education programs (Walmsley & Allington, 1995). Working together to support student achievement in literacy is imperative for ensuring that all special education students receive the appropriate accommodations to reach their full potential.

Although most teachers will be willing and open to meeting during grade-level prep periods, starting and sustaining this process may take time and requires a certain level of administrative support. However, once we were able to establish this routine, grade-level teams took more ownership over the meetings and it became less of a mandate and more of a necessity (see the Student Work Web in Appendix A for a tool that might help establish this routine).

Another ritual or routine that many schools also engage in is the schoolwide walk-through. Walk-throughs normally consist of a general focus or question about instruction that a team—usually consisting of the administration, literacy coach, and a few teachers—utilize to obtain a quick snapshot while walking through classrooms to notice trends in the building. The walk-throughs are quick, normally lasting about 3–5 minutes per class and are not meant to be evaluative or judgmental. The trends can then be shared with staff, and areas to build on for instruction can be identified. These walk-throughs may occur once a month or quarterly to allow teachers to participate and establish routines and rituals that enable teachers to learn from one another and visit other classrooms from different grade levels.

Table 21 presents some other examples of rituals and routines that can be established within a professional learning community to support professional development. Think about the types of job-embedded support provided at your school and routines and rituals that can be established to facilitate this support. The establishment of rituals and routines to support the job-embedded professional development not only helps to create a community and share the responsibility, but teachers are generally very appreciative of routines and rituals that enable them to plan and promote predictability and direction for the goals of the professional

Table 21. Rituals and Routines to Support Job-Embedded Professional Development

Job-embedded professional development within community	Rituals and routines to support professional development
Weekly grade-level meetings on common prep	Agendas identifying the purpose of the meeting, outcomes, and additional support
Modeling lessons in classrooms	Schedule or rotation for modeling; needs assessment given periodically to determine target areas for modeling
Team teaching	Using formative coaching cycle to identify lessons for team teaching
Analyzing student work with an individual teacher or grade level.	Using formative coaching cycle, protocols, and school infrastructure to look at student work

learning community. In addition, as new staff is introduced or schools are beleaguered by teacher turnover, rituals and routines will help to provide the school with a sense of identity and help to weather the storm.

Shared Leadership—Teacher Efficacy

Individual opportunities for professional growth as well as opportunities for shared leadership should also be a priority within the professional learning community. Shared leadership among teachers can be demonstrated through teacher-led professional development workshops, identified teacher leadership roles, and grade-level team leaders. While building a community will enable teachers to be involved in the day-to-day operations of a school and provide feedback for the school's improvement, it is important to note that merely granting teachers greater responsibility for decisions that affect their jobs, such as school policy and curriculum, doesn't guarantee that instruction will improve. However, this also doesn't mean that teacher empowerment is not important. It means that in many settings it is not enough (Kruse et al., 1994). Teacher efficacy or the extent to which teachers believe their efforts will have a positive effect on student achievement (Henson, Kogan, & Vacha-Haase, 2001) will also determine how successful teachers feel as leaders of their classroom and contributors to school communities.

Consider the profiles of two teachers. Teacher A is organized, well planned, and often stays late, long after the dismissal bell has rung. She considers herself an overachiever and takes classes to continue her education. However, year after year the data monitoring of her students' formative and summative assessments indicates that most of her students stagnate in the bottom quartile, not making the academic progress that everyone in the community had expected. Teacher B is not as organized, and sometimes may even be seen as spontaneous or impulsive. Yet she has an excellent rapport with her students and just seems to have an art for making lessons come alive in her classroom. Her teaching practices are a bit unorthodox, yet each year her students show significant progress and demonstrate competency by all measures.

Given the two scenarios, which teacher do you suspect will feel more successful, more motivated, and more capable at the end of the school year? This feeling is often referred to as efficacy. Teachers' sense of efficacy is a judgment about capabilities to influence student engagement and learning, even among those students who may be difficult or unmotivated (Tschannen-Moran & Hoy, 2001), and measures the extent to which teachers believe their efforts will have a positive effect on student achievement (Henson et al., 2001). From our experience, teachers will not believe that their efforts have a positive effect on student achievement if they are not experiencing success or receiving positive feedback.

There are many things that may affect the efficacy of a teacher—one may be their expectations or definition of success; another might be the environment in which they work and the norms established about teaching practice. As literacy coaches, the topic of efficacy intrigued us greatly. We witnessed teachers who worked very hard to meet the needs of their students, yet after talking to them and digging deeper into conversations, they would often admit that they weren't sure if their hard work would actually pay off; oftentimes they doubted their own abilities but felt it a personal obligation to stay late, plan, and "work harder." We couldn't ignore what seemed to boil down to a sense of efficacy that some teachers possessed that helped them to succeed and gave them the courage to try a different technique or approach when the first dozen failed to yield results.

One of the reasons the field of education suffers such a high attrition rate in new teachers is due to a lack of self-efficacy in the classroom. Do higher test scores and student productivity lead to higher levels of teacher efficacy, or is it the teachers' own sense of efficacy that leads to higher test scores and student productivity? Good teaching and positive results in learning is complex. There is no easy formula, and there are no quick fixes. However, no matter what the odds or statistics, one thing we know for sure in our experience: The way teachers feel about their job and how they feel about their students will transfer to the students and will be demonstrated in their ability to teach effectively.

In addition, schools must be very careful not to tie the efficacy of teachers solely to test scores and percentiles. There are many ways coaches can support teacher efficacy, which also supports the relationship with teachers and helps coaches effectively do their job. Teacher efficacy is a win–win situation for everyone. Greater efficacy leads to greater effort and persistence, which leads to better performance, which in turn leads to even greater efficacy (Tschannen-Moran & Hoy, 2001). Helping teachers use formative assessments effectively to monitor progress and collaborating with them to celebrate improvement is a simple, effective way to help build teacher efficacy. Many times teachers don't realize how much a student has grown or how effective a learning activity or teaching technique was because they did not devise a plan for tracking the formative data or create a space for professional reflection. Formative coaching provides the opportunity for the teacher as well as the coach to build efficacy in literacy instruction.

Consider the questions from the self-assessment in Figure 35, used to help support teacher efficacy in literacy, which we gave to our teachers during a schoolwide professional development workshop (see Appendix A for the reproducible Formative Assessment Action Plan). We asked teachers to complete the survey anonymously, and upon completion, we used the data to inform our planning for subsequent whole-group sessions. The results were quite surprising, and in some cases we brought in research and articles to support our staff in some of the areas that might have affected their level of efficacy. While we agree that teacher efficacy is difficult to measure quantitatively, there are ways schools can measure efficacy qualitatively through needs assessments, conversations, and open discussions at school meetings. Teachers who believe that their efforts are not likely to bring about meaningful change, who have lost hope that anything will make a difference in their effectiveness or job satisfaction, are unlikely to be affected by even the best staff development program (Sparks,

Figure 35. Teacher Self-Assessment Form

1. I am able to implement effective strategies to support my most struggling readers.

    Agree   Not Sure   Disagree

2. If I want to learn more about a particular literacy technique or new teaching method, I know what resources to obtain to find the information.

    Agree   Not Sure   Disagree

3. When students fail, I immediately reflect on the strengths and areas of improvement of my own instruction.

    Agree   Not Sure   Disagree

4. Sometimes I feel no matter how hard I try some of the students will always be struggling readers.

    Agree   Not Sure   Disagree

5. I feel comfortable asking for the help I need with literacy instruction in my school community.

    Agree   Not Sure   Disagree

6. I see myself as a leader in my community and often share literacy strategies or new ideas with other teachers.

    Agree   Not Sure   Disagree

7. I feel safe to try teaching new literacy methods in my classroom, even if I don't see immediate results.

    Agree   Not Sure   Disagree

8. I look forward to the results of our school's assessments benchmarks used to monitor my students' progress.

    Agree   Not Sure   Disagree

9. I cannot make students who are not motivated, interested, or committed to learning want to learn in reading.

    Agree   Not Sure   Disagree

10. Some students will just never love reading, and there aren't any strategies, books, or techniques to help these students.

    Agree   Not Sure   Disagree

1983). Schools must consider the efficacy of teachers if they are committed to real reform and want to support the long-term development of teachers.

Step 4: Assess and Celebrate Community Progress

Assessing your community growth and progress and celebrating accomplishments is crucial in sustaining the work of the professional learning community. As your school progresses and deepens its resolve to work together as a community, it is important to establish benchmarks to measure the progress. One way our school celebrated our progress was through our involvement with Partnership Read, which is a standards-based initiative directed by Taffy Raphael of the University of Illinois at Chicago (visit litd.psch.uic.edu/pr/ for more information). Three times a year, schools engage in a gallery walk based on specific target statements or goals in literacy that were developed by each grade-level team. Teams track the formative data and present analysis and findings from the data to the school. Establishing gallery walks provided us with the opportunity to engage in dialogue about our progress as a school and to reflect on what we learned as a community about instruction across grade levels.

Benchmarking progress for celebration is extremely important as schools may sometimes feel as if the community is not progressing at all, but in fact there are small milestones to celebrate. These milestones may be evident in other ways. For example, maybe teachers were willing to meet together on their common planning periods but never actually met and now there are grade levels who meet regularly to discuss student progress and instructional strategies. Maybe grade levels were already meeting but there was no agenda, focus, or outcome for the meetings, and as a result, teachers did not understand how the decisions or conversations in their meetings contributed to the larger goals and vision of the community. Being able to formatively assess the growth of the community enables the coach to tap into specific areas of need and to remind staff of areas in literacy where teachers can learn from one another.

Creating organic opportunities for leadership and identifying teachers on our staff who were willing to help organize and plan professional development were always important goals that we maintained each year. However, the developmental and comfort level of the staff must be taken into consideration. If a community has never looked at student work together, the coach might begin discussing the work of a student with just one teacher or offer to complete a running record for a struggling student and then discuss the next steps within the context of the formative work. Oftentimes we are asked for advice from teachers on meeting the needs of a struggling student or a student who is outperforming peers and needs opportunities for enrichment. How tempting it is for us to just give suggestions without examining the evidence of student learning with the teacher first! However, it is important to do so, as this enables the teacher and coach to build relationships around tangible work and also creates a shared responsibility for the problem solving around the student's needs. Furthermore, if teachers cannot produce evidence of the student's performance, this will spark the conversation about ways this evidence can be demonstrated. Each school may be on a different point of the continuum; however, the coach can provide support to meet the needs of the teacher and students.

Part of the support the coach will provide to help move a school along a continuum requires the coach to understand the history and trajectory of the school community. The assessment of the school community is ongoing and fluid. In addition to assessing the learning community, the coach must also assess and celebrate his or her own professional growth. Questions a coach might ask when assessing the community include

- What progress has our community established since the beginning of the year?
- What examples of shared leadership have helped to support our community goals and vision?
- How do others view my role in the professional learning community? (Am I the expert, the facilitator, the mentor?)
- What small but significant celebrations of student achievement can we have now?

Figure 36 shows the various stages on the continuum of building a school community based on the needs and achievement of the students. Keep in mind that each new member who is brought into the community will need to have an understanding of where the community is developmentally. Likewise, the community will need to adjust to accommodate various levels of understanding that new members may bring.

Figure 36. Stages of Building a Professional Learning Community

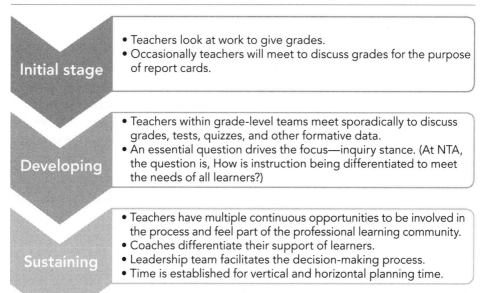

Initial stage
- Teachers look at work to give grades.
- Occasionally teachers will meet to discuss grades for the purpose of report cards.

Developing
- Teachers within grade-level teams meet sporadically to discuss grades, tests, quizzes, and other formative data.
- An essential question drives the focus—inquiry stance. (At NTA, the question is, How is instruction being differentiated to meet the needs of all learners?)

Sustaining
- Teachers have multiple continuous opportunities to be involved in the process and feel part of the professional learning community.
- Coaches differentiate their support of learners.
- Leadership team facilitates the decision-making process.
- Time is established for vertical and horizontal planning time.

In addition, we cannot emphasize enough the importance of the victory lap—celebration. "I know that we have been focusing on analyzing student work and talking about reading strategies to build comprehension and I have learned a lot. Can we just spend our next professional development time celebrating our progress? Can we just take a second to reflect on all the good things we've done in literacy as a school?" These were the words—or more accurately stated, the plea—of a fourth-year teacher during a candid conversation about the upcoming professional development calendar and literacy focus.

An effort to develop a community of trust, openness, and honesty also means that as a literacy coach you will receive feedback that you must take into consideration for future planning—feedback that may not always be the feedback you want to hear. Our initial reaction in our head was, *But we have so much other stuff to do that we haven't gotten to yet! Celebrate? What? We don't have time to celebrate!* But after much reflection and an honest conversation with our principal, we agreed that she was right. We hadn't taken the time to celebrate, to reflect, or to recharge our batteries. Celebrating together and taking the time to congratulate each other and reflect on your progress is an important part of the professional learning community and is necessary for teachers to associate positive feelings with the community. The celebration can be as small as taking the time to have teachers share positive feedback from their classrooms or as elaborate as looking at different forms of data and finding some growth from an individual student or a group of students to illustrate progress. The important part to remember is that all schools have small victories within their communities and these victories should be ritualistic and tied to the goals of the community. In coming up with ideas or ways to celebrate progress, teachers can provide suggestions as well. It is also important for the principal or administration to take part in the celebratory rituals to validate their significance.

Overcoming Inherent Challenges of the Professional Learning Community

Choosing to develop a professional learning community will no doubt present some level of stress or discomfort on the part of a few staff members. However, it is the building of the professional learning community that will enable schools to weather the storm as they implement school change. In talking to literacy coaches locally and abroad at numerous conferences, there were many questions or challenge points that came up specifically as related to the development of the professional learning community. The section that follows discusses three of the most significant questions, or challenge points, that we have heard, as well as our response to those challenges.

Challenge Point #1

I am just the literacy coach. What responsibility do I have in helping to establish a professional learning community around student work, and why can't I just focus on the individual coaching of those who want it?

Our Response

Interestingly, literacy coaches are often in ambiguous roles, particularly when working directly on site in a school—not quite a classroom teacher and certainly not dealing with the myriad issues that affect an administrator. However, it is our assertion that this position also brings great opportunity; because of the ability to understand both sides, the coach ultimately serves as a conduit for change. According to Walpole and McKenna (2004), literacy coaches are the people who are directing continual school improvement work at the state, district, and school levels. We feel that one of the most important aspects of the literacy coach's role is to keep the focus and conversation centered on the learning of the students. The coach is in a perfect position to do this because this role should enable a focus squarely on literacy teaching and learning. Consider the advantages a typical coach might have in regard to supporting the professional learning community and sustaining a focus on looking at student work:

- Access to student work and assessment data schoolwide
- Direct contact with teachers and the opportunity to build relationships with them
- Opportunities to plan or provide direct input to influence professional development
- Some discretion in regard to use of time throughout the day
- A collegial as well as leadership relationship with teachers
- Direct access to the administration
- Access to a network of coaches throughout the district or area
- Access to professional literature, magazines, and Internet forums
- Ability to obtain free samples of various literacy materials to support reading instruction
- Some ability to focus exclusively on the curricular areas of literacy and the opportunity to make connections to other areas across the curriculum
- Access to students and parents
- Understanding of literacy instruction and learning across the continuum of the school

While the coach is in a unique position to support and help build a professional learning community and lead an effort to collectively examine student work to initiate school change, we are not suggesting the coach spearhead this work alone; this work cannot be accomplished devoid of a relationship with the principal, teachers, and other stakeholders associated with the school. The coach must not only be able to connect with the administration but also have outstanding interpersonal and relationship-building skills with the staff at large. We believe the overwhelming majority of teachers and administrators want to be part of a community that is professional, provides opportunities for individual growth, and celebrates their accomplishments, no matter how small. While all of the goals and objectives might not be realized during the coach's time at the school, just as all the students in a classroom might not reach a desired level of proficiency during a given school year, it is in the interest of all parties to put forth the best effort to work toward the common goals and uphold the philosophy of the school. We know this is not an easy task.

Again, literacy coaches must be sensitive to the needs and feelings of others, be extremely diplomatic, and have the ability to communicate effectively. For example, the conversations and communication you have with teachers is paramount to the success or accomplishments of the school. If you implement the suggestions detailed in this book or other techniques that will result in school change, it is very important to think of how you will phrase or convey this information beforehand, particularly in whole-group settings. We have benefited greatly by first showing teachers how this information will help them directly in the classroom and are very careful not to communicate the information as another mandate to add to their to-do list. For instance, consider the language in Figure 37, illustrating how a coach might frame the information from the workshop to teachers and administrators. As stated throughout the book, we believe the role of the coach is to be a catalyst for change. Coaches must be creative and dedicated to supporting the students, administration, parents, and teachers.

Challenge Point #2

How do I balance a focus of looking at student work within our professional learning community considering all of my other duties?

Figure 37. How Coaches Can Frame the Information From Workshops to Teachers and Administrators

I want to share some information with you that I learned from a workshop I attended.	We spoke last week about some questions you had about Sarah's writing. I think I have some information that might be helpful to you. I can assist you in applying the strategies and see if it's something that would benefit your students.
We went to a workshop and the principal has asked me to do a presentation on the information.	I am excited about some information that was shared at a workshop I attended. I'd love to get your feedback on the topic during our next professional development session.
Principal X, can you tell me when you are going to meet with me to discuss the information from the workshop?	Principal X, how can I facilitate the process of getting information to teachers from the discussion at the workshop we attended?
Each grade level is now being asked to look at student work in teams and use protocols to identify trends and meet student needs. What time will your team meet?	I'd like to meet with your grade-level team to share some protocols that might be helpful. Is there a time or day that you are currently meeting that is most convenient for you?

Our Response

One of the most challenging aspects of the job that coaches reported was having enough time to meet with teachers, observe, give feedback, and deal with all of the other paperwork that is often required of literacy coaches. In our experience, organizing the student work as the centerpiece of these conversations has enabled us to work much more efficiently and effectively. When thinking about the levels of intensity from Chapter 4 (see Table 14 on page 94), remember that a focus of looking at student work through formative coaching can be integrated in all levels, depending on where you start. So, for example, if you are at the first level and are simply gathering resources for teachers, you might discuss student work samples and formative data with the teacher to determine what resources would best fit the needs of the students as opposed to ordering a resource strictly because of an advertisement in a popular catalog. The following are 20 examples that we have used in our coaching to build a focus, awareness, and conversation about formative work that would not require large amounts of time:

1. Create a needs assessment to look at how teachers and the school at large are spending their time when not in front of students; look for areas that are ineffective.

2. Create a needs assessment of how coaches spend their time to assess areas of effectiveness.

3. Have bulletin boards in the school that reflect formative student work (names can be removed; grades need not be posted).

4. Always bring student work samples to professional development sessions as a practice to illustrate a concept.

5. Have teachers keep student work folders; bring folders to grade-level meetings and workshops.

6. If a professional development calendar is already established, simply add examples of student work to the agenda to support and illustrate understanding (work doesn't always have to be from the coach's school to illustrate point and could be from other schools or research).

7. Establish exemplars and anchor pieces to display in the building or in coach's office.

8. Carve out time during literacy breakfast meetings to look at one student work sample and pose a question to the participants (work can serve as "mail" or "special delivery" with a note attached).

9. Make student work folders a part of parent–teacher conference so the actual formative work can enter the conversation and parents can see evidence as opposed to only seeing letter grades.

10. Create or develop student portfolios and discuss work in portfolios with other teachers.

11. Create a literacy newsletter that highlights student work that teachers are proud of and that link to school goals and the vision of the professional learning community.

12. Create an archive of student work to use a resource for professional development sessions.

13. Post student work outside of your office.

14. Encourage teachers to keep student work to create their own teaching portfolio.
15. Develop a newsletter or e-mail that focuses on student work and minilessons.
16. Bring student work to meetings with your principal.
17. Encourage principal to have student work as part of observations of teachers.
18. Track individual students' work throughout the year to show progress.
19. Encourage teachers to have student portfolios that include place for student reflection.
20. Encourage teachers to share their "work" (samples, models, etc.) with their professional learning community.

It is important to note that as a literacy coach you will always need to be extremely thoughtful and prudent about the use of a time. However, there are a lot of ways to creatively use your time once you think outside the box and have a connected, underlined focus that you can unify the work you do.

Challenge Point #3

I would like to implement techniques from this book and help support the establishment of a professional learning community, but I don't think I will have my principal's support. They are too _____ (busy, unresponsive, difficult, etc.).

Our Response

Educational research has reinforced the importance of the principal in creating the conditions for an effective school (Smith & Andrews, 1989). Some principals may be new to the concept of developing a professional learning community or analyzing student work and formative assessments as a method of meaningful professional development. Keep in mind that all administrators want to be successful. They want students to achieve, teachers to be productive, and parents to be proud of the school their child attends. If information about professional learning communities and looking at formative data within the community is presented to the principal based on data from the school, research connected to the school's data, and a clear plan of how you will support the process moving forward, in most cases, the administration will be on board to support the effort.

It is also important to have a mechanism to evaluate the process of looking at data collectively to learn from the experience. In some instances, a coach may have to persuade the principal that looking at data (other than test scores) is one of most valuable uses of a teacher's time. To help with this process, we have provided a number of resources and articles below to use during your professional development:

- Black, P., Harrison, C., Lee, C., Marshall, B., & Wiliam, D. (2004). Working inside the black box: Assessment for learning in the classroom. *Phi Delta Kappan, 86*(1), 8–21.

- Black, P., & Wiliam, D. (2004). The formative purpose: Assessment must first promote learning. In M. Wilson (Ed.), *Towards coherence between classroom assessment and accountability* (pp. 20–50). Chicago: University of Chicago Press.

- Stiggins, R.J. (1999). Assessment crisis: The absence of assessment for learning. *Phi Delta Kappan, 83*(10), 758–765.

Due to issues regarding time and other responsibilities, many administrators may need information from these research articles synthesized to convey the most salient points. Principals are required to deal with a plethora of issues, not exclusively related to literacy. However, they may be reassured to know that whatever the direction the school is moving in, looking at student work in an organized way and encouraging teachers to reflect on their practice collectively will result in greater understanding of quality teaching and learning. The key is to start small and develop a relationship with teachers that will help the principal build confidence in your abilities, decision making, and professionalism as a literacy coach. Perhaps you can begin by meeting with one grade level collectively and share the progress and impact of looking at student work with your principal. The following are some additional quick steps to making inroads with your administration:

- Set up regular times to meet with your principal to establish routine check-ins and feedback.
- Make a point to share positive information with the principal about progress of the students.
- If the principal doesn't already attend professional development sessions or grade-level meetings, extend an invitation.
- Ask the principal for feedback about the professional development and listen to his or her suggestions.
- Know your principal and his or her leadership style—is the principal quick with responses and short on time? If so, have information bullet-pointed and concise.
- Is the principal more informal and likely to converse and engage in small talk before getting down to business? If so, start conversations by listening to get a feel for their mood and tone and follow the lead from there.
- Stay professional at all times (avoid gossiping about teachers, parents, etc.) and build the reputation with the principal and teachers that you are there only to build the capacity of teachers and students and that you have their best interest at heart.
- Avoid complaining about how difficult your job is, how teachers are not being cooperative, or how students are lagging behind. If you have a sincere concern about the instruction of a teacher or group of students in a teacher's class, present your concern in the most diplomatic way and exhaust every possible option of connecting and supporting the teacher beforehand, and include how you can further support the teacher or student while stating your concern.
- Be open to feedback from your principal to show that you are reflective and willing to learn.
- Let the principal know how they can support the school. This might include attending or helping to plan the professional development, setting up accountability within the infrastructure, having an open-door policy, and offering feedback from the professional development sessions.

Building a professional learning community is imperative for sustaining schoolwide change. Coaches may use the formative coaching cycle not only to coach teachers individually but also to coach for school reform. Coaches work collaboratively with the administration to support the goals and vision of the professional learning community. Supporting the professional learning community also enables the coach to more effectively support teachers, which in turn will better support academic achievement.

QUESTIONS TO CONSIDER

1. What are the goals and vision for literacy in your professional learning community?

2. How does your community measure the progress toward these goals?

3. What opportunities are provided to promote reflection and the sharing of new ideas?

4. How can job-embedded professional development support the mission and goals of your school?

5. How can you build relationships with your administration and balance this with your relationship with teachers, parents, and students?

6. What added benefits would a thriving professional learning community bring to your school?

CHAPTER 6

Establishing a Winning Record: Coaching for School Change

Imagine This!

Your professional development workshops, cycle meetings, and job-embedded support systems are in place. *Formative coaching*, *professional learning community* and *student work* are all common terms used within your building. Grade-level teams and cycles are meeting regularly to analyze formative assessments and share instructional strategies and techniques. While the community has a lot of room to grow, a foundation for collaboration and professional discourse has been established.

That is when your principal sits you down and shows you the latest writing scores from the students' benchmark assessments in grades 3, 6, and 8.

"The kids are having trouble across the board in the benchmark grades with their writing," he tells you. "It seems like we're missing something in our instruction. We need a plan to address this."

You look at the writing samples from students in the identified grades. At each level, there are large numbers of students who exhibit performance that remains below standard. Clearly, something has to be done.

"I know that some teachers are meeting and collaborating as teams, but I am thinking of just buying a new writing program," the principal continues. "Purportedly, it increases the school's writing scores and will provide the structure and guidance that we need. We can first use the program with the benchmark grades and then branch out to the other grades in the next year or so."

You sit nervously, waiting for the right moment to interject, thinking carefully of how to best phrase your statement.

"Have we had a chance to look carefully at any writing samples?" you ask. "I mean, do we know what the specific concerns are with our students in the benchmark grades as well as the other supporting grade levels?"

He sighs.

"No, I just know according to the printout of the writing scores, we aren't meeting the standards. So this leads me to believe that our kids can't write. We need something quick and effective. We all need to be on the same page, and a writing program will help build cohesion. Plus, with this program I'm interested in, you get the writing booklets and there are teacher guides. Also, if you buy four packs, the following year you get a discount. They will even provide some training on how to use the materials. Ms. Jones said...."

As his voice starts to trail off, you begin to think about what you can do to make sure the kids don't receive a one-size-fits-all writing program as a temporary solution to "fix" the problem for the principal without addressing core student concerns and problems. You empathize with the principal—he's got a difficult job, and he is ultimately responsible for improving student writing. You think about how to address this formatively by looking at the data, the students' writing, and the problems your colleagues have when teaching writing. You reflect on the culture of writing in the school and how the students themselves feel about writing. You wonder if mentor texts are being used to support student writing or if writing is even being taught schoolwide. You start to think about a needs assessment that you could create to give to teachers and students to learn more about their attitude, perspective, and knowledge about writing.

You consider recommending to your principal that this subject be brought before your leadership team to open the discussion and determine what leverage might already exist in your professional learning community to support a schoolwide focus on writing. At this point, you realize the formative coaching model used individually with teachers and small groups must be used schoolwide to improve literacy teaching and learning.

While the school principal will ultimately decide on the direction the school takes in writing, the literacy coach is often viewed as the advisor to the principal or district and likened to a "cabinet member" on literacy. The challenge is ensuring that the leadership team, as well as the teachers, understand the importance of actually looking at student work—not just the numeric data or forms of testing but the actual work that students are producing every day in class. This is not something that can be accomplished at one professional development workshop or during a few grade-level meetings. Rather, the notion of formative coaching and using authentic data to drive instruction must become part of the school's culture and practice so that the school can develop the expertise and skills required to effectively analyze student work in order to identify student strengths, areas for improvement, and instructional strategies.

In this chapter, you will discover how to use schoolwide formative data and action research to initiate and sustain school change. As a literacy coach, one of the most important roles of the position is to provide a context and community that will make change possible. Ask teachers to think critically and deeply about their practice; a scaffold and support system to build the bridge for school change will be paramount. As teachers learn more about themselves individually, they will soon realize they each have an important contribution to make to a larger professional community. They may then have the confidence, purpose, and impetus to not only welcome but also seek out change for school improvement. The coach plays in an important role in negotiating this process and is vital to the success of the change.

Take the example from the opening vignette. The coach might bring a student writing sample to the meeting to facilitate a discussion, such as the sample in Figure 38, an excerpt from a student's persuasive essay on the topic of year-round schooling. Using this example of student work, the group can take a detailed and critical look at the level of progress students are making and target specific areas that may be in need of improvement. There are several different strategies the literacy coach can use in subsequent conversations to broaden the discussion with the principal to support a schoolwide focus of looking at student work in writing. Below are a few ideas:

- Develop a needs assessment that allows teachers to determine how they feel about writing and what specific skills and strategies that students are expected to know.
- Meet with the leadership team to devise a plan to collectively address issues with writing.

Figure 38. Excerpt From Student Essay Brought by Coach to Facilitate Discussion

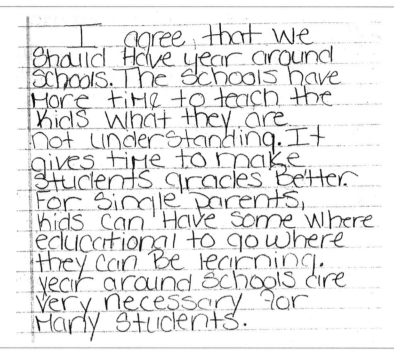

I agree, that we should have year around schools. The schools have more time to teach the kids what they are not understanding. It gives time to make students grades better. For simple parents, kids can have some where educational to go where they can be learning. year around schools are very necessary for many students.

- Form a curriculum committee to focus exclusively on writing.
- Look at the writing standards for each grade level. Give students a preassessment to determine where they are in relation to the standards.
- Bring in research about looking at student writing.
- Look at the writing samples in clusters—primary, intermediate, and upper grades. Determine trends, areas needing more development, and how much time is being spent on writing. Discuss how reading and writing are connected in class and across content areas.
- If the program is something to which your principal is committed, do your own research about the program. Learn it inside and out. Determine how looking at student work can help drive and support the initiative. Consider how the program can be best implemented at your school to meet the needs of your students. Present this

information to your principal as a means of supporting his or her decision.

- Build in time during grade-level meetings or before or after school for looking at student writing; have teachers identify areas of concern and brainstorm next steps.
- Collect monthly writing samples; use protocols to look at samples and give feedback based on samples which are, in turn, based on trends.
- Develop a team to identify common rubrics that can be used in clusters or schoolwide.
- Identify exemplars for the school to look at and set as the standard.
- Discuss the importance of giving students meaningful feedback and multiple opportunities to write.

As we've stated in previous chapters, one of a coach's many roles is creating a context for school change. In the opening vignette, the literacy coach would be acting as a catalyst for change in the writing program. As schools embark on the journey of school change, it is important to note that any new concept—in this case, the possibility of a new writing program—or new drive toward change—even change that others agree will result in a stronger community and better achievement for students—may bring some anxiety. The teachers and the administrators are not the only ones vulnerable to this anxiety; coaches are susceptible as well. However, as a leader it is important to understand school change and remain calm, cool, and poised with knowledge to weather the possible storm. A mantra to remember is to not take the initial reaction of other members in the community personally. Each teacher processes information differently and two questions that most of our teachers seemed to ask themselves as they experienced movement into a new direction were "What does this mean to me?" and "What will I be expected to do?"

If the professional learning community is just being established or is newly established, some teachers still might not even see themselves as a part of the community at all. On the other hand, just the mere notion that a community has been consciously formed and defined may bring stress, as most people understand that with a community comes responsibility, an expectation for contribution, and a shared sense of accountability. The previous chapter was written to underscore the importance of building a professional learning community to engage in the type of deep-level work that is required to sustain school change. It is important to remember that communities are changing, breathing organisms. Consider a neighborhood community. Does it stay the same from year to year? If it did, would it be a thriving community? Most people judge a thriving community by its changes, new landscape, new faces, and obvious development. While it is important for the community to have a foundation and an identity as a small village or town would, it is also important for that community to allow space for growth, development, and innovation. The community cannot thrive to meet the growing needs of its members if it does not continually seek improvement. In this effort to continually seek improvement, however, schools may encounter resistance and obstacles.

How to Get Started

Typically when organizations or teams engage in systematic change, they go through a series of stages. Forming, storming, norming, and performing are four stages of team development that are necessary and inevitable for a team to grow (Tuckman, 1997). Take the example of a school implementing a new writing program. During the forming stage, the school staff is beginning to understand what is being presented and form an opinion or an idea about the task. A new way of thinking is being formed; people are given the opportunity to learn about the changes. In the storming stage (brainstorming), you are bound to have some dissenters: some people might disagree outright with buying a writing program, while others might agree to looking at student work but disagree on what the next step or strategy should be. If a professional learning community has been established, the team will be able to disagree about next steps, ask questions to build understanding, and share honest feedback, while still keeping in mind the needs of the students and the greater good of the community.

Norming is the step where teachers realize that a program is going to be purchased or another approach to dealing with student writing will be implemented. During this phase the expectations will be made clear for them and the new program starts to become a part of the school community. Only once the professional learning community has inherently owned the decision and authentically supported one another in the implementation can the stage move to performing. The chart in Table 22 illustrates how the different stages of the cycle might look with the chapter-opening example of purchasing the writing program.

As your school moves through the change cycle with any new initiatives, it is important to remember that some inherent tension is part of the process. Sharing these stages with the teachers will enable the community to have a name to attach to their reactions, which are often demonstrated as characteristics of the various stages and may also help to build an understanding around school change. Schools may go back and forth through stages or remain stagnant at one stage, never reaching other levels. It may also be necessary for the coach to facilitate the process of moving through the different stages to support the community's growth and development.

Below are some key reminders to keep in the back of your mind when engaging in any kind of systematic, large-scale change:

- Change takes time.
- Some staff members will automatically resist school change no matter what the change is.
- Change must be embedded in authentic work that can be sustained over time.
- Ideas and concerns about change need to be vetted and addressed.
- Change requires strong leadership to implement and follow through.
- Systematic change requires examination of other aspects within the organization and how they will be affected.

Table 22. Four Stages of Team Development

Stage	Description
Forming	Staff begins to understand the direction of the school in writing and learn about the new program.
Storming	Staff may experience some confusion or frustration about the program. Apprehension may set in as well as resistance.
Norming	The writing program is accepted as a part of the school's curriculum. Staff finds a way to integrate the program into their writing block.
Performing	Staff is able to evaluate the effectiveness of the program based on formative data; teachers reflect on student writing and make instructional decisions based on student needs.

Implementing a schoolwide process of analyzing student work and engaging the staff in reflective practice will require an understanding of and familiarity with the characteristics of school change. This will help in times of frustration and also help the teachers understand that change is an ongoing process that requires a strong professional learning community and commitment to be sustainable. Having strategies and techniques to sustain school change and developing a team of teacher-leaders to initiate the effort of collectively examining student work will ultimately change the culture of the school. Grounding the role of the literacy coach in student work will provide you with the opportunity to stay focused on the bigger purpose and larger goal of developing teachers and supporting quality instruction for students.

Providing teachers with the opportunity to look at formative data together, to ask questions, recognize patterns across or within grades, and realize gaps in learning can be one of the most important ways to encourage change. To effectively promote school change and to truly and professionally develop teachers, the process of analyzing students needs to be self-sustaining, long term, and optimally happen with or without the literacy coach present. While the coach can facilitate meaningful conversations during professional development or grade-level meetings, the quality of what is produced in schools is often determined by the quality of the conversations among teachers. *The Constructivist Leader* (Lambert et al., 2002) emphasizes the importance of leading the conversations as a facilitator and the importance of conversations in schools as these relate to school change.

For example, are teachers having meaningful conversations about student work or just surface discussions about what student "can" and "cannot" do? Are coaches having meaningful conversations with principals about the progress of students and teachers or just drilling test score formulas to meet AYP? Are coaches having meaningful conversations with other coaches or just complaining about how their teachers "just don't get it"? Are students having deep-level conversations in classrooms about literature or just general conversations where they mechanically identify the setting, problem, plot, and solution of a story?

Conversations must dig deep to unearth the jewels of knowledge and "aha!" moments waiting to be revealed. Schools can put structures and routines in place to help teachers engage in meaningful conversations.

Once reviewing student work systematically becomes a part of the school's culture and conversations, teachers will also need to develop inquiry and problem-solving skills necessary to collectively and individually implement solutions.

Action Research

While coaches and teachers utilize research from university professors, other classroom teachers, and professional organizations, it is also important to develop teachers in the school who think of themselves as researchers. The role of a teacher is to be the consummate researcher. We ask students to inquire, investigate, problem solve, and apply solutions. The question is, How do we model that as professionals? Helping teachers to understand that they are researchers and that as a school you will be collecting data, examining instructional practices, and coming up with solutions to tackle the problems means that you are engaging in a form of action research.

Let's say that the principal in the opening vignette has agreed to let groups of teachers look at student writing and is open to teacher feedback before making a decision about the writing program. What context might the coach use to frame the work that will be shared? How might the coach structure this process?

According to Watts (1985), "action research is a process in which participants examine their own educational practice systematically and carefully, using the techniques of research" (p. 118). It is based on the following assumptions:

- Teachers and principals work best on problems they have identified for themselves.
- Teachers and principals become more effective when encouraged to examine and assess their own work and then consider ways of working differently.
- Teachers and principals help one another by working collaboratively.
- Working with colleagues helps teachers and principals in their professional development.

Benefits of Engaging in Action Research

As teachers engage in the process of action research, there are a number of benefits that you can expect the team to reap. Most schools will experience a shift in their culture and climate of the professional development simply by engaging in well-organized and productive action research. This shift can be explained by the four benefits (Ferrance, 2000) that result from engaging in action research:

1. Empowerment of participants
2. Collaboration through participation
3. Acquisition of knowledge
4. Social change

Different Types of Action Research

Upon hearing the phrase *action research*, it is possible that some teachers or administrators may become concerned that the school will investigate issues of concern, read about them, and chalk it up as conversation fodder.

> Action research is not a library project where we learn more about a topic that interests us. It is not problem-solving in the sense of trying to find out what is wrong, but rather a quest for knowledge about how to improve. It is about how we can change our instruction to impact students. (Ferrance, 2000, p. 2)

When beginning to think about areas needing literacy improvement in your school, it is important to look at all the data already available at the school, particularly the formative data and student work produced in the classroom. While there are different types of action research, the type of research discussed in this chapter centers around schoolwide action research. Table 23 is a chart that details the different types of action research according to Ferrance (2000).

The Playbook: Implementing a Cycle of Action Research

When engaging in action research, there are five steps (Ferrance, 2000) to be repeated that will help to navigate the process:

Table 23. Types of Action Research

	Individual teacher action research	Collaborative action research	Schoolwide action research	Districtwide action research
Focus	Single-classroom issue	Single classroom or several classrooms with common issue	School issue, problem, or area of collective interest	District issue Organizational structures
Possible support needed	Coach/mentor Access to technology Assistance with data organization and analysis	Substitute teachers Release time Close link with administrators	School commitment Leadership Communication External partners	District commitment Facilitator Recorder Communication External partners
Potential impact	Curriculum Instruction Assessment	Curriculum Instruction Assessment Policy	Potential to affect school restructuring and change Policy Parental involvement Evaluation of programs	Allocation of resources Professional development Activities Organizational structures Policy

Note. From Ferrance (2000).

1. Identifying the problem
2. Gathering data
3. Interpreting data
4. Acting on evidence
5. Evaluating results

After the professional learning community has discussed the purpose and steps of action research they may use the cycle to begin the conversations about writing. Let's take the writing scenario discussed in the opening vignette through the action research process step by step.

Identifying the Problem

The two phrases that we often use at our school to frame discussions when we are working collectively to identify a problem are "I wonder..." and "I noticed...." A teacher might say upon looking at students' writing, "I noticed that students seem to be writing anywhere from a couple of sentences to one paragraph. I also noticed that by the time the students exit third grade they are expected to write a five-paragraph essay based on the goals detailed in the curriculum maps. I wonder how we can encourage students to write more and if there is enough time for students to write during our literacy block. I also wonder if there is a common framework for teaching writing across all grade levels." These "notices" and "wonders" can be jotted down anonymously on poster board for not only the grade level or benchmark cluster grades to ponder but also for the entire staff.

The key is to not approach the problem with a predetermined answer but to earnestly explore and use the school's internal data to make an informed decision about the direction that the school will take. For example, the principal defines the problem as students not meeting the standard in writing. The teachers reflect on their individual data and concur with the principal that the students aren't meeting the standards and are indeed struggling with writing. The coach decides to also ask the teachers to give a needs assessment, which reveals that a large percentage of students do not enjoy the subject of writing during their school day. If the problem is not correctly stated or identified, the data will reveal it.

Gathering Data

After identifying the problem, each teacher is then asked to bring samples of formative data that illustrate the identified problem. This data will also provide evidence of student learning. It is important to note that a variety of classroom assessments may be used to gather evidence of learning (McTighe & Wiggins, 2004). The list that the teachers bring may include

- Writing portfolios
- Journals
- Notebooks
- Essays
- Readers' responses
- Letters

As teachers begin to organize their data and prepare to share them with the group, each teacher looks through samples of the writing data from other classrooms. Teachers jot down notes using the phrases "I wonder" and "I notice" to frame and articulate their feedback. As you organize and facilitate these meetings, here are some important questions to think about to assist the analysis and investigation:

- Are teachers allowing students enough opportunities to produce meaningful data?
- Are we looking at the right data?
- What protocols will we use to facilitate the process of looking at this data?
- How will clusters be organized? Will I, as the literacy coach, facilitate the process as a large group or break the group down into individual grade levels and then meet together as a cluster for grades 3, 6, and 8? Will each grade level need a representative? How will we share our findings with the school?
- What opportunities will teachers have to give feedback about this process? How will I share this feedback?

Interpreting Data

Interpreting data together as a community can be a difficult task; teachers may look at the same student work and find different meanings. Teachers may be unaware of biases they have if the work that is being examined is from their own classroom. If the coach has worked individually with teachers through the formative coaching process and the community has established a professional discourse around examining formative data, schools can begin to deal with the deeper-level work that will result in school change at this step. Using protocols together, determining common language, and establishing a context for job-embedded professional development are detailed in the previous chapters because they are such critical elements to schools' being able to make systematic shifts in literacy teaching and learning.

As the teachers examine the student writing, they come to an agreement about the following in their findings:

- Some students write so little that teachers are not able to confidently make inferences and hypotheses about their writing.

- When students do write enough, their writing does not reflect specific traits of the identified genre.

- Students have problems with the organization of their writing, regardless of the type of formative assessment.

As you listen to teachers during the meetings and ask clarifying questions, you realize that the teachers across grades 3, 6, and 8 do not share a consistent meaning of the writing process. For example, one teacher shares that she sometimes skips the brainstorming or prewriting process and has the students "jump right in" to their topic. Another teacher shares that she believes she needs to take students through the writing process together over a specified number of days. Finally, another teacher shares her model of writing workshop that might include one student working on a single piece for several weeks while another student completes that same piece in a matter of days. This data is extremely valuable to you as a coach; it informs specific job-embedded professional development for individual teachers and helps the community decide on the best next steps for the school based on real formative data from the students, as well as the teachers, while taking into account the school's available resources, vision, and goals.

Acting on Evidence

All of the preceding information is evidence for the community to consider. The action or next steps is the critical element that will ultimately lead to the change. The team, along with the support of the administration, decides to do the following:

- Agree to provide students with the opportunity to write daily for a specific period of time as a part of the literacy block

- Consistently teach the writing process with a common language and focus

- Make conferring with students a regular part of the writing time to get feedback from students and understand their motivations, frustrations, and feelings about writing
- Provide exposure to genres through multiple opportunities, such as using mentor texts, doing shared writing activities, consistently modeling writing for students, and providing writing examples for students

After looking at this list, it is obvious that the school could have taken a different direction or as a coach you may have other thoughts about how the school can act on this evidence. The important thing to remember is that schools must design a systematic, transparent, and research-based process for deciding next steps as opposed to exclusively choosing a next step based on a flier in the teacher's mailbox from an outside professional development company or on a new program being marketed from the latest writing guru. While it may be overwhelming for the coach and the school to think about how to act on the evidence, we have included a template to help schools organize the work (see Figure 39 for a sample of the Formative Assessment Action Plan, and see Appendix A for a reproducible version).

The Formative Assessment Action Plan in Figure 39 includes a focus question based on action research steps. The problem that the school identified can simply be stated in the form of an inquiry-based question, and schools might use the rest of the template to help organize and clarify the work that has been established so far. When writing your focus question, it is important to identify a problem area that will be meaningful and realistic within the context of the teachers' daily work and responsibilities. According to Ferrance (2000), the question should

- Be a higher order question (not a yes/no question)
- Be stated in common language, avoid jargon
- Be concise
- Be meaningful
- Not already have an answer

The action plan contains eight components, which were used with various school districts to support the work of the literacy coach around

Figure 39. Formative Assessment Action Plan

Focus question	How can we encourage our students to enjoy writing while building their capacity to meet the standards in writing for their respective grade level?
Integration with other content areas	Reading, social studies, science
Target group	3, 6, 8
Goals and outcomes for initiative	Students will partake in the writing process daily and produce work based on grade-appropriate standards. This work will include writing portfolios, journals, and personal biographies. Teachers will implement minilessons based on student needs and allow daily time for extended writing, conferring, and sharing or reflection. Teachers will utilize information from a student writing interest survey.
Strengths existing currently in professional learning community	Common grade-level preps, one restructured professional development day after school, teachers willing to meet once a week before school, professional journals about writing, support from coach, importance placed on integration of content areas across the curriculum, protocols for looking at student work, school knowledge of the six traits of writing.
Specific professional development goals and job-embedded support	Coach will provide grade-level and cluster professional development around the writing process as well as ideas for minilessons. Coach will create needs assessment to determine frequency of writing in classroom and pedagogy of writing. Coach will meet with teachers to look at student work in writing and support teachers based on needs.
Method for charting progress	Teachers will keep portfolios of student writing. Teachers will identify rubric to assess student writing and systematically give feedback to students. They will log information from student–teacher writing conferences. Teachers will give needs assessment and interest survey to students at the beginning of the action plan and again at the end of the quarter to assess feedback from students about writing.
Evaluation and celebration	Teachers will share insights, reflections, and progress with each other. Teachers will share specific strategies that they've learned that will support coherence schoolwide. Coach will log meetings with teachers and reflect on progress with coaching and supporting students in writing.

formative assessments. The purpose of the components was to support the community in identifying a focus question to frame the plan and to ensure that there are specific outcomes for the teacher, the students, and the coach to support the inquiry. Coaches may choose to use the action plan initially with a small cluster of teachers and eventually use the plan schoolwide to support large-scale change. The schoolwide action plan will help facilitate the process of looking at student work collectively as a community.

Each step in the action research process lends itself to job-embedded professional development for the entire school and enables the coach to authentically support students and teachers. Building a professional learning community with a strong administrative team is a crucial factor when implementing formative coaching for schoolwide change. As school communities reflect on their progress and commit to working together to increase student achievement, there are virtually no limits to what they can achieve.

Evaluating Results

Evaluating the results of the data is one of the most important steps of the process and often one of the steps forgotten. Evaluating the data closes the gap of the cycle and seals any progress toward success. There are many ways schools can evaluate the data from the action plan. The section that follows describes two structures that we have used at our own school successfully. Having these structures also enables us to reflect on our progress and to continue the cycle of effective instruction and formative coaching.

Data Wall. A data wall is a quick way to display the progress and data in a particular area of the school. For example, at our school we have a data wall that charts the running record progress of students from grades K–5. As a school we formally commit to implementing running records four times a year (see Figure 40). This data is tracked and charted on a wall by reading levels using the Fountas and Pinnell leveling system. In addition to the running record levels, the wall also includes the standardized test data of the previous year, as well as data from the Scholastic Reading Inventory for grades 4 and 5. The purpose of the data display is for us to reflect as a community on our progress and to view student learning on

Figure 40. Data Wall

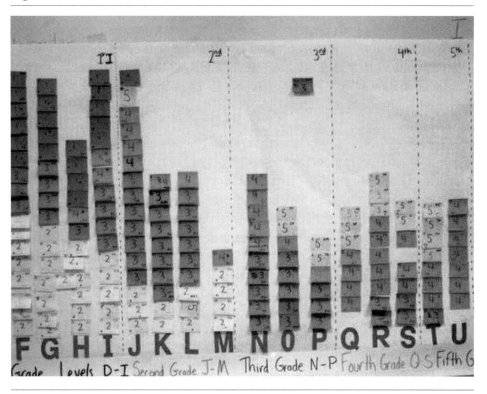

a continuum. The wall does not contain the teacher's name or homeroom number or the students' names. All of the information on the wall is categorized by grade level, and we encourage teachers to bring in and track other formative data to display.

Read-Through. The idea of a read-through came as a more authentic companion to our schoolwide walk-through. In addition to our principal enabling each teacher to participate on the schoolwide walk-through at some point in the year, we also engaged in school read-throughs. During this time, a group of teachers would read through the work of an anonymous group of students, identifying trends and strengths in the work. Sometimes we might be looking for very specific traits, depending on our focus as a school. For example, if we are looking for the use of higher order thinking questions on teacher-created assessments and are assessing the type of questions and the student responses, we might look at random samples of assessments and discuss the type of questions and responses as a way to evaluate our progress toward that goal. The idea to remember also is that as a community you are looking to celebrate evidence of progress. As you evaluate your initiatives, it is very important to look for improvement, regardless of how slight. These tiny morsels of improvement will motivate, encourage, and revive the dedication of the community.

REFLECTING AND EXTENDING

To build instructional coherence and see the impact of your role schoolwide, there must be systems in place for schools to collectively examine and discuss student work. Here are a few reminders as you begin planning with teachers.

- Research articles about school change.
- Familiarize staff with action research and its benefits.
- Make a decision to look at student work collectively as a school to improve literacy teaching and learning.
- Look at various protocols to support reflection and analysis; find ones that your school is comfortable using.
- Choose a plan to sustain analysis of student work schoolwide; start small if necessary.
- Provide opportunities for teachers to share concerns, questions, and comments; be flexible based on their needs and understandings.

QUESTIONS TO CONSIDER

1. What experiences or strengths do you already possess to help lead a schoolwide effort on looking at student work? What leverage already exists within your school?

2. How do you feel this collective focus will affect student achievement and learning in literacy? What challenges might you face as you embark on this focus?

3. What techniques or strategies will you utilize to deal with issues of time and management around a collective schoolwide focus?

4. How can the use of protocols further support the effort of looking at student work?

5. What strategies or techniques would you have implemented differently as the literacy coach after reading this chapter?

6. How can you build a support network with other coaches in your district? What personal plans or goals do you have for your own professional development as a literacy coach?

CHAPTER 7

The Legacy of Your Coaching

Imagine This!

You are attending a literacy coach network meeting for your school district. There are literacy coaches from six other sites, and you are learning about some new materials and strategies for teaching reading that the district would like to share. The facilitator allows for a 10-minute break, and you catch up with a coach that you used to attend class with in graduate school. He asks you how things are going and you tell him exceptionally well. You tell him that you are meeting regularly with teachers to discuss their practice and have been asked to model more lessons this year in teachers' rooms than in the past. You also share with him the intense focus on looking at student work collectively and the progress the school community has made overall toward achievement.

"I have heard a lot about the good things going on at your school. I am glad that you are seeing some improvement. So what's the one thing you think that's really turned it around?" he asks.

"I don't know if it's one thing," you say slowly as you think carefully about your response. You want the response to sound attainable, but you don't want to undermine the necessary efforts made by your school to sustain the changes. "We have a great principal and very dedicated teachers. I think the biggest added value is our commitment to looking at student work and really having the courage to dig into all types of data, specifically formative data, and not shy away from the various interpretations that the data yields."

Sounding a little more interested, he asks, "How do you guys meet to look at all this formative data? We barely have time to go through the standardized test data that we receive at the end of the year."

"After school, before school, during professional development days. We have communities of teachers that use ongoing data as a part of their everyday practice so it's ingrained in the lessons, conversations, and culture in our building. We have a process for looking at data schoolwide on a macrolevel as well. I also use the data to stimulate our coaching conversations, modeling sessions, and team teaching. We just use what's already being produced in a meaningful way and build transparency around the purpose and intent of our analysis."

"Wow, that sounds great." He nods his head slowly in approval. "I try to meet with teachers at each grade level, but it isn't really working that well. Plus, next year it is possible that I will have more than one school site—I don't know how I will tackle that. I also encourage teachers to bring in data during our meetings when we have them. Sometimes the teachers don't have any work to bring and other times when they do bring work we end up talking about something else. Then I get overwhelmed and I think, Is it my job to do all this? I have offered to do modeling and team teaching at the beginning of the year, but so far not many teachers have taken me up on it. I just wish there was a 'way in.'"

You nod and smile knowingly, "There is."

As the tools and strategies from this book are shared with one coach, many other coaches will begin to think about their trajectory and prepare for how their role might change from year to year. The information in this book was written to provide the literacy coach with a game plan and road map that will be useful regardless of the impending changes he or she may face. In addition, all of the strategies and techniques outlined in the book can be used with any instructional leader seeking to implement school change. In fact, our hope is that teachers become so proficient and skilled at looking at their formative data and the community and culture becomes so deeply rooted in student achievement and outstanding literacy instruction that our teachers become formative coaches who guide other teachers in using student work to determine the course of instruction, curriculum, and their own professional development (Nidus & Sadder, 2009).

In our role as coaches, each year our duties and responsibilities shifted a bit from the previous. However, as we became more comfortable and effective in our role, the demands became more pronounced, expectations became more defined, and the call for student achievement more clear. While the role of the literacy coach in general has evolved over the years, the prominence and prevalence of the literacy coach model owes much to the Reading First and Striving Reader initiatives of No Child Left Behind

(Cassidy, 2007). With a new U.S. federal administration, many ask what will become of the literacy coach position and those who support teachers with literacy instruction? Our effort to root our support in the analysis of student work and base our decisions in the formative data has enabled us to adjust to the changes, validate our contributions, and find stable grounding for our relationships with teachers. The concept of formative coaching is one that will stand the test of time, regardless of the federal administration or mandates from the government.

Rolling With the Punches

Because so much depends on funding and resources, it is difficult to predict exactly how the role of the literacy coach might change on a national level or even at a school level. However, there are a few scenarios that have already changed the look and feel of the role of literacy coaches in schools, some of which we have experienced ourselves and have been shared by coaches that we've interviewed. When thinking about how the role of the coach might change, some extended responsibilities that might have to be considered for those who want to stay in the coaching position are outlined in the following sections.

District-Level Coaching

Many school districts are employing area coaches or district-level coaches and moving away from the onsite-based coaching model. In Chicago, where we are employed as coaches, the area or district-level model has become more popular, as fewer schools have a school-based literacy coach. Think of the opening vignette. The teacher shared that he would be required to work as a district-level coach for the next year. How could he use the information from this book to be an effective coach with multiple schools if he already acknowledges that he is struggling at one school?

The following suggestions and steps from the previous chapters in the book would still apply. First the coach would need to develop a relationship with the staff at the schools he serves and, most importantly, the principals at each school. The coach will need to find out the goals at each school, how the principals and district see his role, and, equally important, how the role is explained to teachers at each school. The bottom line for him will be how he can serve and support the schools to which he is assigned. Using formative data from teachers and students will be even more important because he will have less time to pick up the nuances and dynamics of the school.

Next, the coach would need to work diligently at keeping the lines of communication open with all partnering schools. Follow-up is important for coaches who work at the school level but absolutely imperative if you are an area or district coach. A coach may decide to start a newsletter to keep in touch and provide links to online resources or research that schools can use. Passing on materials or samples that might be helpful is always an excellent way to keep in contact. When visiting schools, it is important to have data on hand about the school and to seek the feedback and input of teachers and administrators to make sense of the data. You might offer to lead or copresent a professional development session based on a needs assessment or on specific areas of concern highlighted from the data. The formative coaching cycle can apply, even if you do not report to the same school each day. The cycle will give teachers and principals a sense of predictability for your visits and will give them a way to conceptualize your support. When discussing student work, it will be extremely important to use protocols to help facilitate and maximize meeting times.

One of the most important things to remember if you are a coach in several schools is that you may have to work that much harder to establish relationships and build trust. Your disposition, attitude, and interactions with the staff will be looked at much more closely, and you may be seen as an outsider or bureaucrat no matter how sincere your intentions. Because your communication with the teachers and administrators may not be as frequent as you'd like, it is paramount that your interactions are meaningful, pleasant, and productive.

Curriculum Coaching

While our school always included in its mission the commitment to supporting the professional development of classroom teachers, we recently expanded this mission to include resident teachers. Through the Academy of Urban School Leadership (AUSL), our school has taken on a dual mission that includes training residents for successful teaching in high-needs urban populations. The residents in the program already have a bachelor's degree, sometimes in areas other than education, and complete a yearlong residency at a training academy. Our school is designated as a training site, and in preparing our residents for teaching, our goal is to establish effective educators in all areas across the curriculum in addition to literacy.

In order to support our mentor teachers and residents at our own site, our role has included coaching teachers in areas in addition to literacy. Talking to teachers about formative assessments in math, science, and social studies has given us the opportunity to learn more about the pedagogy and philosophy of our teachers as it relates to curriculum in general, and it also helps us to develop a more integrated approach to teaching, which translates into a better learning experience for students. Even though we are both certified to teach math, science, and social studies, we still needed to conduct a lot of research and seek outside help to further build our understanding of the content areas and how they support each other at each grade level in our building. Figure 41 illustrates an example of student work used during a curriculum coaching discussion connecting the social studies and reading content areas. We supported the teacher in using reading strategies to help students visualize the buffalo in their social studies unit of westward expansion. Our background and understanding of the formative coaching cycle enabled us to begin coaching teachers in these areas because the foundation was rooted in the work of the students and aligned to the state standards and goals, with which we were very familiar. We created communities of teachers within our school and across the AUSL network to support one another for specific teaching strategies and techniques within the content areas, and we committed to learning more about areas in which we had limited understanding.

As a result of our expanded roles, we were able to further build our professional learning community and obtain a better understanding of the challenges teachers faced across the curriculum. Working as a coach in an elementary school usually affords the opportunity for a literacy coach to exclusively focus on the area of reading because most teachers have a reading block in their schedule. However, as our school moved to a more departmentalized model in the upper grades, we look more like a high school, and as a result, we had to come up with creative schedules and infuse literacy into other subject areas. This helped to us to develop professionally as coaches and to build an understanding of how literacy was being incorporated in other subject areas. Teachers began to see the

Figure 41. Student Work Used for Curriculum Coaching Discussion

Name **Darell**

The Buffalo

Strategy Focus: Visualizing

<u>Directions</u>: Listen and visualize as I read the passage about buffalo.

(V+)

1. List the <u>describing</u> words that you hear that help you create a mental picture of a buffalo.

It's so big, It was a millions *maybe* six feet high and ten feet long, He can weight up to two thousands pounds, Short neck, and rounds shaudlers, brown fur, a beard that gcos to his chin, two short horns that cure out from his Fore Head

2. List the <u>action</u> words that explain how buffalo move or what they do.

Wondering around the grass, they tat on grass, Yell, roar, fight, crash, snort and bellow

have a short tail

Nice describing action words!!

3. Using your describing words and action words, draw a picture of what you visualized while I read (draw a picture of what you think a buffalo looks like).

4. Compare and contrast your drawing of a buffalo with the picture of the buffalo.

the horns the same, are beer-is the same, Are tails is different, are legs is different. I was a lump thats the same.

explain how they are different

200

need to plan with a more integrated approach, and our reflection time was spent looking at the experience of a school day through the eyes of the students, transitioning from one subject area to the next. While our primary focus and expertise is still in the subject of literacy instruction, often we wonder how it was we didn't look at or ask about the other subject areas to build a better understanding about teaching and learning in general in our school. We understand now that literacy instruction doesn't happen in a vacuum.

Coaching With Targeted Student Support

"This position is first and foremost an adult support role. We do not want someone to simply come in and pull out the students who are struggling. Rather we are looking for someone who can coach, train, and support teachers in the classroom so that they can build the necessary skills in their toolbox to help all of their students. Differentiation has to be the key in delivering instruction to meet the needs of the students and delivering quality professional development for the varying capabilities of our teachers." These are the words of a former NTA principal during an interview for the literacy coaching position. While focusing on providing support to adults as a priority has mainly held true over the years, our position has included more direct support to students as we've grown as a school.

However, the support we lend to students is in conjunction with the teachers, as opposed to a teacher sending us a student to take in a small room down the hall and work our magic to improve their reading. When we do work with a student, our next step is always to engage the teachers in conversations about the work we will be doing, and we look at the data and have numerous conversations with the teachers about the students before we assess them or pull them for an intervention.

Most of our interaction with students involves assessments. This might take place in the form of running records or basic reading inventories. We work side by side with teachers to plan instruction for individual students and model the techniques we use with them. In some circumstances, we might regularly see a student over an extended period of time in order to monitor progress. What we have found that doesn't work is pulling out a student sporadically, not having conversations with teachers about the student, being unaware of what type of instruction is going on in the classroom with the student, and taking weeks to even identify or diagnose the student's difficulty. This, however, is what happens in many schools across the United States. Our goal in any situation is to empower the teacher to use the same techniques we are using within the context of the classroom community. This gives us the perfect opportunity to team teach and model lessons so that we can illustrate how the teacher will accommodate the needs of a particular student, given that they may have 20 other students with completely different needs. The formative coaching cycle is used effectively in the same way when working with students to provide targeted support as teachers are helping to facilitate the progression through the cycle.

Working with targeted students on a regular basis also gives us the opportunity to put instructional strategies into practice across various grade levels. Often we might introduce a technique in a professional development session that theoretically can work with all grade levels, but we haven't had the opportunity to actually try it out with each age group. As a result of working directly with the students, we are able to put specific strategies into practice that also enable us to hone our professional development based on the real needs of the students that sit in front of the teachers we support.

Finally, pulling out students has also given us the opportunity to learn with the staff. Teachers began to see us not only as an instructional leader but also as a fellow colleague, as we share our frustrations, concerns, and "aha" moments with them. Each year our school engages in many initiatives for reading, which naturally lend themselves to pulling students to do work around literacy.

For example, each year we engage in a young authors project where students write books and learn about the process of becoming a published author. We often will pull out students to develop their manuscript, and we model lessons in classrooms about the writing process. We also work with students in preparation of our annual spelling bee, and we often pull students for our annual museum walk, which is a schoolwide curriculum focused on celebrating and reflecting on the culture of our students. Initiatives involving coaching, standards implementation, and grant requirements have been instrumental in bringing coaching to the forefront (Jay & Strong, 2008). The more rituals and routines the professional learning community has in place, the more authentic opportunities the coach will have to work with students and add depth to their role as a coach.

Your Legacy

Take a second to think about it. What would happen if you didn't return to your position next year and your role was without a replacement? What systems do you think still would be in place that you helped to create? Which teachers are you sure you have influenced? What legacy would you leave behind in the lives of the students? While the coach is obviously one piece of the school puzzle, much research and buzz has circulated about the literacy coaching position. Over the last few years, several literacy coaching books have been published, numerous authors and consultants have been hailed as literacy experts, and various websites and discussion forums have been established that focus squarely on the role of the literacy coach. As a coach, think about the impact you want to make while you are in your role and what you want the community to be able to do without you should you leave your role. One of our colleagues once said her goal is to literally work herself out of a position. She wanted to build such strong leadership teams and such a deep understanding of literacy instruction at her school that the school community itself would be able to sustain and implement the practices that she put into place. This has often been one of our goals as well: The hallmark of our success is evident in the leadership we help to promote among teachers and in the urgency and commitment we are able to build around literacy within our community.

Why We Coach

Vince Lombardi, a highly successful football coach, once said, "The achievements of an organization are the results of the combined effort of each individual." Coaching is not a job that can be done alone. It is not an effort that can just be dictated by the administration and handed down to teachers. Successful coaching takes a sincere belief in teamwork, an honest journey of reflection, and an unwavering commitment to excellence. The coach must not only display these characteristics individually but also inspire others to express them as well. When done effectively, coaching can transform an entire school and affect the professional trajectory of every teacher in the building.

In addition, according to the Literacy Coaching Clearinghouse (www.literacycoachingonline.org), four major changes in teaching have been cited by instructors as a result of literacy coaching. The first change is becoming willing to try more things in the classroom, another is using more authentic means of assessing students' needs, the third includes the modification of instruction based on students' needs, and the final change includes adapting teachers' beliefs and philosophy based on the educational theory and research they've read. We have seen all of these changes with several teachers at our school in our role as coaches. Yes, the job is difficult and comes with more challenges than triumphs and seemingly more setbacks than breakthroughs. However, each stumbling block can be used as a steppingstone and as an opportunity for professional and individual growth. Coaches must celebrate their baby steps as well as their milestones. The progress, feedback, and compliments from each teacher, student, and administrator must be relished. To further understand the impact of coaching, we've asked teachers to talk about their experience of being coached and how this has contributed to their professional growth. Here are some of the comments we received:

> Having a coach has helped me implement various reading strategies across the curriculum. My students are able to read a variety of genres and still use the same skills we've learned in professional development to build comprehension. The coaching I have received has also given me the opportunity to see lessons demonstrated in my classroom, which has helped me as well as my students. The communication in the building has improved so much because of the literacy coach.
>
> —Marlene Tyler
> Third-grade teacher

> At first, I didn't realize there was a benefit to having a literacy coach in the building.... It has been great having such knowledgeable individuals to go to for support. I don't think I would have been as effective in my teaching. There are some things that I didn't have a clue about and having the opportunity to be a part of the professional development has definitely provided many "aha" moments. Although there is still a lot for me to learn, I am definitely a better teacher because of the knowledge I've learned through coaching and professional development.
>
> —Lyntina Lampley
> Sixth-grade teacher

> Having a coach has helped me so much in my teaching. The most important thing my coach ever told me was to keep an archive of student work that I can look back on to measure the progress of my students. Sometimes I would get so discouraged. But I would look back at how far they came and I would think about the words of encouragement my coach always had to say when

we would meet to discuss student work and our balanced literacy block. Those conversations really helped to keep me going. I am in school now to be a literacy coach because of the experiences I've had with coaching.

—Anita Orozco
Special education teacher

While the feedback and encouragement from teachers is excellent, it wouldn't be complete without knowing exactly how coaching has directly affected our students. As stated by Fisher (2007), "Change should be the outcome of coaching. That change might be defined in terms of teacher behaviors or student learning or both" (p. 4). Below is an example of our most coveted example of feedback—and the most compelling reason why we coach. This was shared by one of our teachers from a student's reflection sheet:

This year has been a great year. I have learned so much. I think the part I like best about this year is how my teacher helps me. Last year I knew I wasn't doing that well but it would be during report card pick-up time that I would know what I needed to do to get my grades up. Now I know how I am doing all the time. My teacher sits with me and talks to me about my work. I keep a folder with all my work. This really helps me stay organized. We also do a lot of fun projects and my teacher tells us to do our best, its not all about getting an A but what you learn while you are doing the work. Everything I turn in my teacher actually looks at and we get to share our work or she gives us a chance to talk with her about our work. Sometimes Ms. Sadder and Ms. Nidus come in to help our class and my teacher. I think it's cool to have different people teaching you because you learn more. My teacher says she loves to learn too. My grades are better than before. I love to read now and I love my teacher.

REFLECTING AND EXTENDING

The role of the literacy coach may change in the near future. It is important that coaches position themselves to be relevant and effective for years to come. Research supports the effectiveness of literacy coaching, and universities across the nation have a large number of graduate students interested in literacy leadership positions. Coaches must be committed to their own professional development. Formative coaching enables the coaches to stay current and roots their support in the tangible and meaningful evidence of student learning.

QUESTIONS TO CONSIDER

1. If you are currently a literacy coach, how might you anticipate any changes to your position? What might you do to prepare yourself for the changes?

2. If you left your position today, what legacy would you leave behind? If you are not currently in a literacy coaching position, what legacy would you want to leave behind after you left a school?

3. How would you prepare for the difference between a districtwide coach and a school-based coach? What could the different types of coaches learn from one another?

4. How will you get feedback from teachers about your effectiveness? How will you measure and celebrate your own progress?

Reproducibles

The Formative Data Analysis Cycle

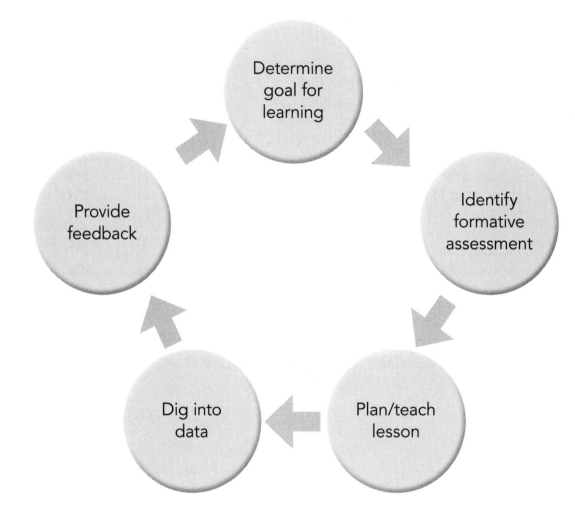

Exploring Your Role as Coach

What are my responsibilities as a coach?

Outside the domain of the coach

Reflecting on Relationships

Names of teachers	Relationship rating	Strategies I've tried	Strategies I will try in the future

A. List the names of teachers that you are responsible for working with during the year and rate your coaching relationship with them.
- Established coaching relationship (4–5)
- Developing coaching relationship (1–3)

B. Note the strategies that you have employed for developing a coaching relationship with individual teachers:
1. Working with a group of students in teacher's classroom
2. Helping to collect/analyze data about student(s)
3. Study group—Discussing professional literature
4. Supporting with resources
5. Classroom modeling
6. Coteaching
7. Lesson planning
8. Notes that provide feedback on lessons
9. Scheduling meetings to provide feedback on lessons
10. Providing teacher with opportunity to visit other classrooms
11. Working with teacher in grade-level group

Grade-Level Data Inventory Form

Grade level	Quarter 1	Quarter 2	Quarter 3	Quarter 4
Comprehension				
Word knowledge				
Fluency				
Writing				

The Literacy Coach's Game Plan: Making Teacher Collaboration, Student Learning, and School Improvement a Reality by Maya Sadder and Gabrielle Nidus. © 2009 by the International Reading Association. May be copied for classroom use.

Schoolwide Data Inventory Planner

Grade	Assessments Q1	Assessments Q2	Assessments Q3	Assessments Q4
Grade				
Grade				
Grade				
Grade				
Grade				

Note. Use code to delineate type of assessment (some assessments may have multiple categories): C = comprehension; W = writing; F = fluency; O = oral; L = listening skills; W = word knowledge.

The Literacy Coach's Game Plan: Making Teacher Collaboration, Student Learning, and School Improvement a Reality by Maya Sadder and Gabrielle Nidus.
© 2009 by the International Reading Association. May be copied for classroom use.

Looking at Student Work Check-In

What type of work will we look at? When did students do this work?

Under what circumstances did students do this work?
- ❑ Independently
- ❑ In groups/pairs
- ❑ With teacher support
- ❑ Varied depending on learner

What is your goal in looking at this work? What do you particularly want to discuss?

Do you have rubrics, criteria, or checklists that you use to assess this work?

Scripting Tool

Focus: _____

Time Period: _____

Teacher: _____

Grade: _____

Names of focus students (if applicable): _____

Start Time: _____

End Time: _____

Teachers	Students

Analyzing Scripting Data

I notice	
I wonder	

Types of Talk Tool

Choose a time interval to observe. List names/initials of students if known. Number statements so that you know the order of discussion.

Code the statements after observation: HQ = higher order questions; LQ = literal questions; RB = responses that build on others' statements; TS = textual support; NC = negative comments; P = praise; R = redirection.

Teacher talk	Student talk

Collaboration Planner

Type of support: Class: Date: Time:	
Focus of the lesson	**Materials needed**
Formative information to collect/observe	**Role of coach**
Role of teacher	**Students/groups to be made aware of**
Follow-up (teacher)	**Follow-up (literacy coach)**

Coach Planning Sheet for a Think-Aloud

How did you decide on the plan? How did you decide on the activity?

What were you concerned about when planning? How did this affect your choices?

Did you make plans to differentiate your instruction? How?

What were you noticing while you were teaching? What questions did you have?

Were there any particular students who stood out during the lesson? Why?

Did you make any instructional decisions during the lesson based on the feedback you were receiving from the students?

What kind of "at a glance" formative data were you using? What kind of deeper-level data do you think you could use to analyze student understanding?

What do you think worked about your lesson? How do you know?

Record of Coaching Activities

Name of teacher	Date	Date	Date	Date	Date	Date	Date	Date	Date	Date	Date

Level 1	Level 2	Level 3
Analyzing formative data = AF Resources = R Checking in = CI	Lesson planning = LP Coteaching = CT Observing/collecting data = Obs Meeting with team = Me	Providing feedback = F Demonstration lesson = D Teachers sharing = TS

The Literacy Coach's Game Plan: Making Teacher Collaboration, Student Learning, and School Improvement a Reality by Maya Sadder and Gabrielle Nidus.
© 2009 by the International Reading Association. May be copied for classroom use.

Coaching Clip

1. Observations

2. Considerations

3. Celebrations

Feedback Stems

Questions to promote reflection on data
• Let me share the data I took while I was in your class. What questions do you have after seeing this?
• Can you choose a sample where you think a student really understood _____? Why was this student successful?
• Let's look at the work of the student. What do you see here that is a strength? How can we build on this?
• What measurable goals and outcomes can we set for this student? How can I help you monitor their progress and support them?
• What do you think the data shows about ____? How can you use it in your planning?
• What does this formative assessment ask students to do? What are the subskills they need to have?
• How should we look at this data?
• What would you expect this work to look like for a __-grade student? Why do you say this?
• What criteria do you use when you look at _____?
• How do you take into account this group of learners in your planning?

Questions to promote reflection on teaching
• I noticed that you did _____ in the lesson. Can you tell me about that?
• Talk to me about your lesson. What were the objectives and goals of the lesson? How was this articulated to students?
• What do you think students learned after the lesson? How do you know?
• Can you tell me about some of your students' learning needs? How do you know this?
• What are some ways you differentiated your teaching?
• What were you thinking while you did _____?

Conversation stems for when teachers are feeling frustrated
• So there seem to be two key issues you are discussing.
• So I hear several themes emerging.
• Considering _____, what are some tangible things I can help you with ____?
• What type of support can I provide you to help you with _____?
• I understand your frustration and know that you are doing the best you can to meet the needs of the students. Can you talk to me about areas where you see progress despite the difficulties you have faced?
• What I hear you saying is….
• What do you think would happen if…?

Grade-Level Project Planning Guide

Purpose of the project

Outcomes

Protocol for planning

Dates for professional development planning

Guide for planning activities/agenda

Agendas must include (not necessarily in this order):

o

o

Guide for 20-minute presentation

Student Work Web

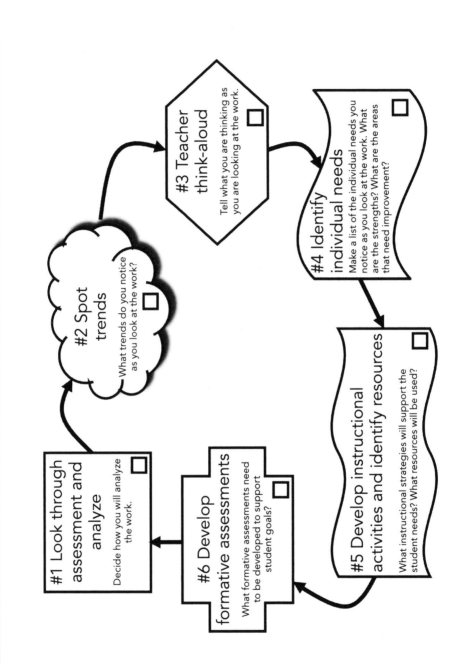

#2 Spot trends

What trends do you notice as you look at the work?

#3 Teacher think-aloud

Tell what you are thinking as you are looking at the work.

#4 Identify individual needs

Make a list of the individual needs you notice as you look at the work. What are the strengths? What are the areas that need improvement?

#1 Look through assessment and analyze

Decide how you will analyze the work.

#6 Develop formative assessments

What formative assessments need to be developed to support student goals?

#5 Develop instructional activities and identify resources

What instructional strategies will support the student needs? What resources will be used?

The Literacy Coach's Game Plan: Making Teacher Collaboration, Student Learning, and School Improvement a Reality by Maya Sadder and Gabrielle Nidus.
© 2009 by the International Reading Association. May be copied for classroom use.

Formative Assessment Action Plan

Focus question	
Integration with other content areas	
Target group	
Goals and outcomes for initiative	
Strengths existing currently in professional learning community	
Specific professional development goals and job-embedded support	
Method for charting progress	
Evaluation and celebration	

Protocols

Trendspotting Organizer

	Trends among group (strengths/challenges)	Implications for instruction	Notes on group progress
Members of Group 1			
Members of Group 2			
Members of Group 3			
Members of Group 4			

The Quick Sort Protocol

Goal

This protocol can be used by a coach to analyze student work either with one teacher or in a larger group. The coach and teacher might choose to focus on a particular part of the protocol rather than go through all of the steps.

1. The work: Discuss the formative work that you have chosen.
   a. What is the purpose of this formative work? How does it relate to grade-level goals or standards?
   b. Did students work together or individually?
   c. What type of scaffolding did the teacher provide? Was the assignment differentiated for certain students? If so, how?

2. Criteria: The teacher should describe how the work will be evaluated.
   a. What evidence of learning did you hope to see in this work?
   b. How will you evaluate student work? (rubric, checklist, exemplar, previous work done by students, other)

3. Quick sort: Sort the work.
   a. The coach and teacher should discuss how to examine the work. What can you look for quickly when analyzing the work?
   b. Take a brief amount of time to examine the work and make three piles. For example, you might make piles based on students whose work seems below standard, on-target, and above standard for that grade level.

4. Analyze: What do students have in common in this group?
   a. What are strengths that you see in this group? Identify examples.
   b. What are areas that are challenging for them? Identify examples.

5. Reflect
   a. Is this formative assessment a good way of evaluating student knowledge or skills?
   b. Do the students understand the purpose of this assignment?
   c. Do students know how their learning is being evaluated? Do they know what good work looks like?

6. Plan: Based on your discussion, what type of instruction does this group of students need?

7. Repeat steps 4–6 for other groups of learners that have not yet been analyzed.

The Literacy Coach's Game Plan: Making Teacher Collaboration, Student Learning, and School Improvement a Reality by Maya Sadder and Gabrielle Nidus. © 2009 by the International Reading Association. May be copied for classroom use.

Class Impressions Protocol

Purpose

To look at a variety of related formative assessments from a class in order to gain insight from multiple data sources

Materials

At least two different types of formative assessments to address a similar skill or understanding

Time

Two meetings

Procedure

1. What are you going to assess? (Meeting 1)
   a. To start the meeting off, the facilitator should introduce the purpose of the protocol.
   b. Next, the teacher begins by discussing the learning goal and describing why it is important for learners.
   c. The facilitator should write down this goal and save it for the next meeting.

2. How will you assess it? (Meeting 1)
   a. As a team, consider various ways to assess the learning goal. How can different formative assessments shed light on student understanding of this goal?
   b. How can you make sure students understand the goal?
   c. What are the underlying skills students need to have to be able to do well at this learning goal?
   d. Are there any classroom observational data that can be collected that would be helpful in understanding your learners?
   e. How can you accommodate students with different learning styles?

3. How can I organize the data? (Preparation for Meeting 2)
   a. Prior to the next meeting, the teacher should enter the formative data for students into the Classroom Impressions Template.
   b. For each formative assessment, the teacher should determine which category it fits into and color-code accordingly: above (green), on (yellow), or below (red). (Other categories might be applicable.)

4. How can I make sense of the data? (Meeting 2)
   a. Start the meeting by reviewing the learning goal.
   b. With samples available, the teacher should quickly run through the administered formative assessments and under what conditions this goal was assessed. For example, were students working in teams? Independently? The teacher should also explain the criteria for the categories. How did the teacher decide which color to code a particular assessment?
   c. Quick glance: The coach and the teacher should take a few minutes to look at the assessments to get an overview of the assessments.

(continued)

Class Impressions Protocol (continued)

d. Analyze the code: The teacher should choose a perspective to look at the data that best fits his or her goal.

Bird's-eye view: If the teacher wants to see how the whole class fared, she can look at the template as a whole and answer the following questions.

Vertical view: If the teacher wants to see how students did in one assessment, she can look at a single column and answer the following questions.

Zoom in: If the teacher wants to understand how one student fared, she can look across that student's data for assessments.

- What color dominates?

- What is the least frequent color?

- What assessment seemed the most challenging for students? Why?

- Are there any assessments that the teacher thinks are invalid measures of the learning goal?

- Choose a sample of student work to investigate more deeply. What do you notice?

Reflection

The facilitator should lead the team through the process of reflecting on the assessments and instruction. Each member can make suggestions on how instruction might be differentiated for learners.

1. Process

2. Product

3. Content

4. Learning environment

Class Impressions Template

Directions: After filling in the formative data, color-code the information and begin to look across and within assessments.

Learning goal					
Student	Formative assessment	Formative assessment	Formative assessment	Formative assessment	Formative assessment

Note. green = above standard; yellow = on standard; red = below standard.

The Literacy Coach's Game Plan: Making Teacher Collaboration, Student Learning, and School Improvement a Reality by Maya Sadder and Gabrielle Nidus. © 2009 by the International Reading Association. May be copied for classroom use.

Goal Setting—Individual Student Analysis Method (ISAM)

Purpose

This technique allows teachers to monitor progress and set goals for individual students.

Time

At least two meetings

Meeting 1: Gathering Formative Data

1. Teacher explains why the student has been brought to the attention of the coach.

2. Data overview: Have the teacher choose various types of data that analyze different aspects of literacy to bring to the meeting.
   a. Fluency data
   b. Running records
   c. Writing
   d. Comprehension assessments
   e. Spelling assessments

3. Teacher can start by describing the learner:
   a. Attitude toward learning
   b. Home support
   c. Enthusiasm
   d. Habits

4. Teacher and coach spend 10 minutes looking through the work and jotting down strengths and challenges based on what they see.

5. The teacher and coach then begin by describing their impression of the learner based on the work. Each time a statement about the learner is made, it should be backed up by evidence from the work.

6. Choosing a learning goal: The teacher talks about learning goals for this student.
   a. Are there smaller goals contained within the larger one?

7. Selecting a formative assessment: The teacher chooses a formative assessment to progress monitor. The teacher explains:
   a. Why is this data important?
   b. How often will they collect this data?
   c. How will the data be evaluated?
   d. What is the goal for the student in a determined period of time? What do you expect to see? With whom should you share this data?

(continued)

Goal Setting—Individual Student Analysis Method (ISAM) (continued)

8. Planning instruction: Next, the teacher and coach can think about what lessons will help the student demonstrate his/her learning in this area. It is also important to address how the teacher can accommodate to the student while taking into account realistic challenges such as time constraints, grade level expectations, and needs of other students.

9. Reflect: The teacher and coach should make an appointment to reconvene to look at the progress of the learner.

Meeting 2: Analyzing Progress

1. Teacher should restate why the student was originally brought to the meeting.

2. Dig into data: Begin by analyzing student work for specified formative assessments. Line up similar assessments chronologically. Spend time looking at work.
   a. Look at oldest assessment and compare to newest. Is there evidence of progress? If so, what are areas of improvement?
   b. Has the student met the goal that you set for learning?
   c. What areas does the student still need to develop? Can you break down this assignment into smaller steps or chunks for the learner?
   d. What lessons do you think were helpful to the student? How do you know this?
   e. Were other areas related to this skill affected? If so, how?

3. Feedback: Discuss how the student was provided feedback.
   a. How have you let the student know about his or her learning goals? What was the context of this situation?
   b. With whom else did you share this goal and progress? How did sharing with these people affect student progress?
   c. How often did the student receive information about his or her progress? What was his or her attitude toward this learning goal? Did his or her attitude change during this period of time?

4. Evaluate: Decide on future learning goals based on student progress.
   a. Discuss next steps.
   b. Do you need to choose another learning goal, continue with the one you have selected, or gather more information on the student?

Individual Student Monitoring Template 1

Name: _____

Assessment type	Strengths	Challenges

What will I continue to monitor? How often will I assess?

What are my goals for this student in the given time period?

What criteria will I use to judge progress?

Instructional techniques to try

How will I provide feedback to the student (and family) about progress? How often will I do this?

Individual Student Monitoring Template 2

Name: _____

	Assessment 1	Assessment 2	Assessment 3	Evidence of progress
Strengths				
Challenges				

Focus areas	Instructional ideas/curriculum	Ways to provide feedback

New goal

The Literacy Coach's Game Plan: Making Teacher Collaboration, Student Learning, and School Improvement a Reality by Maya Sadder and Gabrielle Nidus. © 2009 by the International Reading Association. May be copied for classroom use.

BEST Assignment Analysis

1. Describe it

    a. Teacher describes nature of assignment (formative assessment) to group and describes the context of the assignment.

    b. Group or coach can then ask follow-up questions about the context of the assignment.

2. Questions to ask

    a. What was the purpose of the assignment? How does it connect to goals/standards for this grade level?

    b. Was the work done independently or collaboratively?

    c. Was the assignment differentiated? How?

    d. Were parts of this assignment scaffolded by the teacher? If so, how?

3. Break it down: As a group, brainstorm the steps that students need to take to be successful with this assignment. Put steps in order if applicable.

    a. What subskills were contained within this assignment? "To complete this assignment successfully students need to be able to..."

    b. Are there certain concepts, vocabulary, or strategies that would help them perform successfully on this assessment?

4. Make a plan

    a. **B**reak it down: What minilessons around the subskills can help students demonstrate their knowledge for the assignment?

    b. **E**xemplars: How can I provide examples (or models) of what good work looks like?

    c. **S**chedule it: Where in my day can I provide students with the practice they need? When can I give them feedback on their progress?

    d. **T**rack it: How will you monitor students' progress? What will be effective ways you can provide feedback about their progress?

The Literacy Coach's Game Plan: Making Teacher Collaboration, Student Learning, and School Improvement a Reality by Maya Sadder and Gabrielle Nidus. © 2009 by the International Reading Association. May be copied for classroom use.

BEST Assignment Analysis Template

Assignment type	
Goal of assignment	
Break it down • Subskills contained within assignment • Important vocabulary/ concepts to teach	
Exemplars • What kind of models/ examples can I provide for students to know what good work looks like?	
Schedule it • When will I teach these skills (subskills)? • When will I provide feedback?	
Track it • How will I monitor my students' progress? • How will I provide feedback about this?	

REFERENCES

Allen, J. (2006). *Becoming a literacy leader: Supporting learning and change.* Portland, ME: Stenhouse.

Allington, R.L. (1993). Michael doesn't go down the hall anymore (Literacy for all children). *The Reading Teacher, 46*(7), 602–604.

Arkansas Department of Education. (2006). *What is job-embedded professional development?* Retrieved June 30, 2009, from ideas.aetn.org/pd/what_is_job-embedded_professional_development

Astuto, T.A., Clark, D.L., Read, A.-M., McGree, K., & Fernandez, L. deK.P. (1993). *Challenges to dominant assumptions controlling educational reform.* Andover, MA: Regional Laboratory for the Educational Improvement of the Northeast and Islands.

Black, P., & Wiliam, D. (1998). Assessment and classroom learning. *Assessment in Education, 5*(1), 7–74. doi:10.1080/0969595980050102

Cassidy, J. (2007). Literacy coaches: Here today, gone...!!!??? *The Literacy Professional, 17*(3), 1–2.

Colton, A.B., & Sparks-Langer, G.M. (1993). A conceptual framework to guide the development of teacher reflection and decision making. *Journal of Teacher Education, 44*(1), 45–54. doi:10.1177/0022487193044001007

Dole, J.A. (2004). The changing role of the reading specialist in school reform. *The Reading Teacher, 57*(5), 462–471. doi:10.1598/RT.57.5.6

DuFour, R. (2004). What is a "professional learning community"? *Educational Leadership, 61*(8), 6–11.

DuFour, R., DuFour, R., Eaker, R., & Many, T.W. (2006). *Learning by doing: A handbook for professional learning communities at work.* Bloomington, IN: Solution Tree.

DuFour, R., & Eaker, R. (1998). *Professional learning communities at work: Best practices for enhancing student achievement.* Bloomington, IN: Solution Tree.

Ferrance, E. (2000). *Themes in education: Action research.* Providence, RI: Brown University. Retrieved March 30, 2007, from www.alliance.brown.edu/pubs/themes_ed/act_research.pdf

Fisher, D. (2007). *Coaching considerations: FAQs useful in the development of literacy coaching* [Brief]. Denver, CO: Literacy Coaching Clearinghouse. Retrieved August 10, 2009, from www.literacycoachingonline.org/briefs.html

Fountas, I.C., & Pinnell, G.S. (2001). *Guiding readers and writers: Grades 3–6.* Portsmouth, NH: Heinemann.

Friend, M., Reising, M., & Cook, L. (1993). Co-teaching: An overview of the past, a glimpse at the present, and considerations for the future. *Preventing School Failure, 37*(4), 6–10.

Garmston, R.J. (2000). Glad you asked. *Journal of Staff Development, 21*(1), 73–75.

Hatch, J.A. (2002). Accountability shovedown: Resisting the standards movement in early childhood education. *Phi Delta Kappan, 83*(6), 457–462.

Henson, R.K., Kogan, L.R., & Vacha-Haase, T. (2001). A reliability generalization study of the teacher efficacy scale and related instruments. *Educational and Psychological Measurement, 61*(3), 404–420. doi:10.1177/00131640121971284

International Reading Association. (2004). *The role and qualifications of the reading coach in the United States* (Position statement). Retrieved June 18, 2009, from www.reading.org/downloads/positions/ps1065_reading_coach.pdf

Jay, A.B., & Strong, M.W. (2008). *A guide to literacy coaching: Helping teachers increase student achievement*. Thousand Oaks, CA: Corwin.

Joyce, B.J., & Showers, B. (1995). *Student achievement through staff development* (2nd ed.). White Plains, NY: Longman.

Kluger, A.N., & DeNisi, A. (1996). The effects of feedback interventions on performance: A historical review, a meta-analysis, and a preliminary feedback intervention theory. *Psychological Bulletin, 119*(2), 254–284. doi:10.1037/0033-2909 .119.2.254

Knowles, M.S. (1990). *The adult learner: A neglected species* (4th ed.). Houston, TX: Gulf Publishing.

Kolb, D.A. (1994). Learning styles and disciplinary differences. In K.A. Feldman & M.B. Paulsen (Eds.), *Teaching and learning in the college classroom* (pp. 151–164). Needham Heights, MA: Ginn.

Kruse, S.D., Louis, K.S., & Bryk, A.S. (1994, Spring). Building professional community in school. *Issues in restructuring schools, 6*, 3–6. Retrieved June 30, 2009, from www.wcer.wisc.edu/archive/cors/Issues_in_Restructuring_Schools/ISSUES_ NO_6_SPRING_1994.pdf

Lambert, L., Walker, D., Zimmerman, D.P., Cooper, J.E., Lambert, M.D., Gardner, M.E. et al. (2002). *The constructivist leader* (2nd ed.). New York: Teachers College Press.

Langer, G.M., Colton, A.B., & Goff, L.S. (2003). *Collaborative analysis of student work: Improving teaching and learning*. Alexandria, VA: Association for Supervision and Curriculum Development.

McTighe, J., & Wiggins, G.P. (2004). *Understanding by design: Professional development workbook*. Alexandria, VA: Association for Supervision and Curriculum Development.

Mehrabian, A. (1972). *Nonverbal communication*. Piscataway, NJ: Aldine Transaction.

Nanus, B. (1992). *Visionary leadership: Creating a compelling sense of direction for your organization*. San Francisco: Jossey-Bass.

Nidus, G., & Sadder, M. (2009). Learning from student work. *Educational Leadership, 66*(5). Retrieved June 30, 2009, from www.ascd.org/publications/educational_ leadership/feb09/vol66/num05/Learning_from_Student_Work.aspx

Pearson, P.D., & Gallagher, M.C. (1983). The instruction of reading comprehension. *Contemporary Educational Psychology, 8*(3), 317–344

Raphael, T.E., Highfield, K., & Au, K.H. (2006). *QAR now: Question–answer relationships*. New York: Scholastic.

Rasinski, T.V. (2003). *The fluent reader: Oral reading strategies for building word recognition, fluency, and comprehension*. New York: Scholastic.

Schön, D.A. (1983). *The reflective practitioner: How professionals think in action*. New York: Basic.

Schön, D.A. (1987). The crisis of professional knowledge and the pursuit of an epistemology of practice. In C.R. Christensen & A.J. Hansen (Eds.), *Teaching by the case method: Text, cases, and readings* (pp. 241–254). Boston: Harvard Business School.

Smith, W.F., & Andrews, R.L. (1989). *Instructional leadership: How principals make a difference.* Alexandria, VA: Association for Supervision and Curriculum Development.

Sparks, G.M. (1983). Synthesis of research on staff development for effective teaching. *Educational Leadership, 41*(3), 65–72.

Toll, C.A. (2005). *The literacy coach's survival guide: Essential questions and practical answers.* Newark, DE: International Reading Association.

Toll, C.A. (2008). *Surviving but not yet thriving: Essential questions and practical answers for experienced literacy coaches.* Newark, DE: International Reading Association.

Tomlinson, C.A. (1999). *The differentiated classroom: Responding to the needs of all learners.* Alexandria, VA: Association for Supervision and Curriculum Development.

Tschannen-Moran, M., & Hoy, A.W. (2001). Teacher efficacy: Capturing an elusive construct. *Teaching and Teacher Education, 17*(7), 783–805.

Tuckman, B.W. (1997). *Theories and applications of educational psychology.* New York: McGraw-Hill.

Walmsley, S.A., & Allington, R.L. (1995). Redefining and reforming instructional support programs for at-risk students. In R.L. Allington & S.A. Walmsley (Eds.), *No quick fix: Rethinking literacy programs in America's elementary schools* (pp. 19–44). New York: Teachers College Press.

Walpole, S., & Blamey, K.L. (2008). Elementary literacy coaches: The reality of dual roles. *The Reading Teacher, 62*(3), 222–231. doi:10.1598/RT.62.3.4

Walpole, S., & McKenna, M.C. (2004). *The literacy coach's handbook: A guide to research-based practice.* New York: Guilford.

Watts, H. (1985). When teachers are researchers, teaching improves. *Journal of Staff Development, 6*(2), 118–127.

Wildman, T.M., & Niles, J.A. (1987). Reflective teachers: Tensions between abstractions and realities. *Journal of Teacher Education, 38*(4), 25–31.

Wood, F.H., & McQuarrie, F., Jr. (1999). On-the-job learning. *Journal of Staff Development, 20*(3), 10–13.

INDEX

Note. Page numbers followed by *f* and *t* indicate figures and tables, respectively.